A Guidebook for Aspiring Meteoriticists

The 50 State
UNOFFICIAL
METEORITES

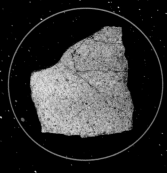

Schiffer **Kids**

4880 Lower Valley Road, Atglen, PA 19310

YINAN WANG

This book is dedicated to my daughter Naia. – Yinan Wang

"Schiffer Kids" and the Schiffer Kids logo are registered trademarks of Schiffer Publishing, Ltd.
Amelia logo is a trademark of Schiffer Publishing, Ltd.

Designed by Danielle D. Farmer
Cover design by Danielle D. Farmer
Type set in Ranchers/Vag Rounded/Optima Reg

ISBN: 978-0-7643-6508-9
Printed in India

Published by Schiffer Kids
An imprint of Schiffer Publishing, Ltd.
4880 Lower Valley Road
Atglen, PA 19310

Phone: (610) 593-1777; Fax: (610) 593-2002
Email: Info@schifferbooks.com
Web: www.schifferbooks.coms

For our complete selection of fine books on this and related subjects, please visit our website at www.schifferbooks.com. You may also write for a free catalog.

Schiffer Publishing's titles are available at special discounts for bulk purchases for sales promotions or premiums. Special editions, including personalized covers, corporate imprints, and excerpts, can be created in large quantities for special needs. For more information, contact the publisher.

FSC MIX
Paper from responsible sources
FSC® C018179
www.fsc.org

THE 50 STATE FOSSILS,
A GUIDEBOOK FOR ASPIRING PALEONTOLOGISTS
Yinan Wang | Illustrations by Jane Levy
978-0-7643-5557-8 | 10"x7" | 72 pp. | 168 images | $18.99

THE 50 STATE GEMS AND MINERALS,
A GUIDEBOOK FOR ASPIRING GEOLOGISTS
Yinan Wang | Maps by Jane Levy
978-0-7643-5995-8 | 10"x7" | 72 pp. | 168 images | $18.99

CONTENTS

INTRODUCTION

Occasionally, we look up and see shooting stars. It's a moment of awe and wonder that encourages us to make a wish. Every so often, a larger meteor will light up the sky. When that happens, it is possible for bits of the meteor to make their way down to Earth. When found, these bits are called meteorites. Meteorites are fascinating objects from space. They can be studied to learn about the history, chemistry, and geology of asteroids and, rarely, the Moon and Mars too. Meteorites are important to us here on Earth, and this book will explore some of the more interesting meteorites that have been found in each state.

What makes these unofficial is that no state currently has an official meteorite. Perhaps one day, one of these meteorites may become an official state meteorite.

WHAT ARE METEORITES?

A METEORITE IS A NATURAL OBJECT FROM SPACE THAT LANDS ON A PLANET'S SURFACE.

Space may seem to be mostly empty, but in fact there are many natural objects moving around, such as comets, asteroids, and meteoroids. When these objects enter Earth's atmosphere, they become heated from hitting air molecules at high speed,

The Goose Lake meteorite from California

which makes them bright and visible as meteors. Those that survive the passage through the atmosphere and reach the surface of Earth (or another planet) are considered meteorites. Unnatural objects, such as satellites, that fall to Earth are not meteorites; they are considered "space junk." A scientist who studies meteorites is a meteoriticist.

WHERE DO METEORITES COME FROM?

THERE ARE MANY OBJECTS IN SPACE THAT CAN EVENTUALLY TURN INTO A METEORITE. THE MAIN ONES ARE ASTEROIDS, METEOROIDS, COMETS, AND PIECES OF PLANETS.

ASTEROIDS

Asteroids are natural objects in space; they range in size from 1 meter (3 feet) wide to almost 1,000 kilometers (620 miles) wide. Early in the history of the solar system, there was a lot of dust and debris. Some of this dust started collecting together due to gravity; this accumulation of matter got bigger and bigger until it formed planetesimals. Some of these

The asteroid 4 Vesta

planetesimals grew large enough to become planets, such as Earth and Mars. Other planetesimals became large enough to have hot interiors with metal cores but not big enough to be considered planets. Most asteroids are smaller planetesimals or fragments of larger broken-up planetesimals.

Asteroids can be made of a variety of materials. Many contain small, round particles of rock called chondrules and also contain a lot of iron-nickel. Some are entirely iron-nickel, and others are a variety of minerals. There are an estimated 1.9 million asteroids bigger than 1 kilometer (0.6 mile) located in the area between Mars and Jupiter. This area is known as the "asteroid belt." Asteroids can also be found farther out in space or closer to Earth. Some "near-Earth" asteroids end up becoming meteorites.

METEOROIDS

Meteoroids are natural objects in space that range from 2 millimeters (0.07 inch) to 1 meter (3 feet) in size. Objects smaller than meteoroids are called micrometeoroids. As with asteroids, meteoroids can be made up of a variety of materials and may be small fragments of asteroids or

Comet Neowise

planets. Most meteoroids that enter Earth's atmosphere will burn up as meteors, but a few may land on the ground as meteorites.

COMETS

Comets are objects in space that are mostly made of ice, dust, and small rock particles. Comets range in size from 500 meters (1,600 feet) long to 100 kilometers (60 miles) long. When they are heated by the sun, they produce gases. The gas around a comet is called a coma, and the gas trailing behind it is called a tail.

Comets usually come from an area called the Kuiper belt, beyond the orbit of Neptune, or they may come from even farther, from the Oort Cloud. They fall toward the sun because of its gravitational pull and then swing out again into space. Their orbits can take hundreds of years or longer to complete.

Yearly meteor showers are caused by Earth passing through debris from a comet's trail; for example, the Perseid meteor shower is the result of debris from the comet named Swift-Tuttle. Meteor showers are spectacular but do not produce meteorites, because the debris is too small and completely burns up in the atmosphere, never reaching the ground. However, comets have likely hit Earth in the past, and any surviving piece would count as a meteorite. It is believed that a lot of Earth's water came from comets.

PLANETS AND MOONS

Occasionally, the planet Mars gets hit by large asteroids. These impacts may be strong enough to blast pieces of the planet into space. These pieces drift around in space as meteoroids and asteroids until they cross paths with Earth and land as Martian meteorites. These special meteorites are confirmed to be from Mars because of their chemistry. The same thing happens on the Moon; large asteroids hit the Moon and knock off pieces that make their way to Earth. Martian and Lunar meteorites are very rare.

A meteorite on the planet Mars, found by the Curiosity Rover in 2016

METEORS AND FIREBALLS

When an object in space begins to enter Earth's atmosphere, it is usually traveling very fast, sometimes greater than 12 miles per second (45,000 miles per hour). Earth's atmosphere is made of air molecules, and a fast-moving object hitting air molecules will generate heat. When an object is hot enough, it will start glowing, also called incandescence. This bright, glowing object makes a streak across the sky, and that's what we see as a meteor. Meteors are usually seen in Earth's atmosphere about 75 to 120 kilometers (45 to 75 miles) above the ground. Most disintegrate from heat and colliding with molecules when they're still 50 kilometers (30 miles) up.

A fireball is a meteor that is brighter than usual. According to some definitions, a fireball is brighter than any planet. Fireballs also tend to be larger objects that enter the atmosphere. They are bigger and brighter and last longer than most meteors—they can last for tens of seconds or longer and may explode. Fireballs are more likely than other meteors to result in meteorites because they are usually big, so there's a better chance they will have fragments that reach the ground. Extremely large fireballs are referred to as bolides. These will often result in meteorites and may also damage structures on the ground.

A meteor in the sky, next to the Milky Way

A stamp commemorating a fireball in 1947 that produced the Sikhote Alin meteorite

FEATURES OF METEORITES

METEORITES USUALLY HAVE FEATURES THAT MAKE THEM STAND OUT FROM EARTH ROCKS. SOME OF THESE FEATURES ARE EXPLAINED BELOW.

FUSION CRUST

When a meteorite falls to Earth, it gets heated up in the atmosphere, and parts of it melt off. This results in a thin, dark crust called a fusion crust. Freshly fallen meteorites look like they have been burned. Fresh fusion crust is usually black or a dark color, sometimes with cracks and occasionally with lines called flow lines. Sometimes it is slightly shiny and when broken will reveal a lighter-colored interior. When fusion crust is exposed to the elements, it becomes less dark. All meteorites that are found should have some kind of fusion crust.

The Creston meteorite covered in fusion crust

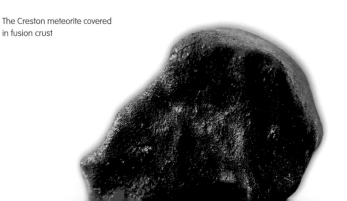

REGMAGLYPTS

Regmaglypts are dimples and dents on the surface of a meteorite. When a meteorite is falling through the atmosphere, it gets heated up and pieces melt off or are knocked off in a process called ablation. Dimples and dents are formed by ablation of the meteorite's surface. Sometimes these are called "thumbprints." Not all meteorites will have regmaglypts, but some will be completely covered with them.

A meteorite from Antarctica with regmaglypts

DENSITY

Meteorites tend to be denser than average Earth rocks. If you pick up a meteorite and compare it to an Earth rock of similar shape and size, the meteorite will feel heavier. That is because most meteorites contain some iron, which is heavy. Iron and stony-iron meteorites are extremely dense from their high metal content. Because they're denser than normal rocks, many meteorites end up being used as doorstops before people realize what they are. Not all meteorites are dense, though. A few rare carbonaceous meteorites are lighter than average Earth rocks.

The Holbrook meteorite with fusion crust; it is denser than average rock

ORIENTED SHAPES

As a meteorite travels through the atmosphere and gets ablated, it will often take on an aerodynamic shape. Most often, this causes one side of the meteorite to be more rounded than the other. Sometimes the rounded side is a dome or is cone shaped. Sometimes the entire meteorite will take on a football shape. This rounded shape can show how the meteorite was oriented as it came through the atmosphere. As a result, we say that these meteorites have orientation.

An oriented meteorite, with flow lines

IRON-NICKEL CONTENT

Most meteorites contain some iron-nickel alloy. Often, there will be little flecks of iron-nickel on the surface and throughout the interior of the meteorite. Some meteorites contain significantly more metal; they may even be entirely metallic. Because of their iron content, magnets will be attracted to meteorites and stick to them. Their metal content also allows metal detectors to detect most meteorites. However, not all meteorites contain metal, and therefore a rare few will not be picked up by a magnet or be sensed by a metal detector.

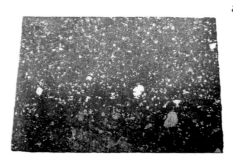

Flecks of iron-nickel in a slice of the Flandreau meteorite

METEORITE HUNTING AND COLLECTING

After a meteorite lands on Earth, many people will be interested in finding the meteorite, including scientists, hobbyists, and dealers. Finding a meteorite is difficult and time consuming. Meteorite hunting usually involves two categories: falls and finds.

FALLS

Large meteors and fireballs that become meteorites and are seen or detected by

Freshly fallen Creston meteorite still in the field

people are called falls. In the past, tracking down a fall relied on finding people who witnessed the meteor and asking them which direction the meteor was going or where the sound of explosions came from. Curious locals who witnessed a meteor hitting the ground may go to find it themselves. Today, since many people have video cameras and scientists have sky-monitoring cameras, captured imagery helps provide trajectory information to suggest where a meteorite might or did land. Doppler radar is used for weather monitoring but can pick up the trail from large fireballs and debris.

Meteorite hunters will use all this information and usually show up in the area of a fall within a day or two. They begin hunting using metal detectors, since most meteorites contain some amount of metal. Sometimes they find a meteorite by sight because it stands out against the area's usual background.

FINDS

An old meteorite find in the desert

Meteorites that fell without being witnessed but are then still located are called finds. Many meteorite hunters look for meteorites in places where they are more likely to find one. Meteorites tend to weather into dust quickly in warm, wet regions, but they can survive for hundreds of years in drier areas.

So meteorite hunters prefer to look in dry areas, such as a desert. They use metal detectors to find rocks with a higher metal content, since these may be meteorites. Meteorite hunters also visit dry lake beds where meteorites stand out against the flat terrain. Internationally, scientists go to Antarctica and find meteorites on the ice sheets, where there are no other rocks. Meteorites are often found on farmland by farmers who hit them with their plows and notice they're different from other rocks.

SIDE NOTE:

Permission from the landowner is needed before hunting for meteorites on private property. In the US, meteorites belong to the landowner, so an agreement must be made to decide who will own the meteorite after the find. Meteorite laws on federal and state lands vary, so always check first before going hunting. It is illegal to collect meteorites in national parks and national monuments.

NAMING METEORITES

All documented meteorites get named. When one is found, it is named after a nearby permanent feature that is commonly used on maps. In the United States, meteorites are usually named after nearby towns or counties. Sometimes meteorites can be named after mountains, lakes, parks, and historical sites. If meteorites from different falls are found in the same area, their names may be followed by a number or letter. It is often believed that meteorites should be named after the nearest town with a post office, but this is a misconception.

organic compounds that provide clues to the origin of life. The Tenham meteorite of Australia contains high-pressure minerals that scientists speculate could be found deep in Earth's mantle. The Lafayette meteorite from Indiana is an example of a Martian meteorite that allows us to study Mars's rocks.

When someone finds a meteorite, scientists require them to donate a portion (20 grams or 20 percent, whichever is smaller) for study before making the meteorite official. This way, science has samples of every official meteorite.

A specimen of the
Allende meteorite

METEORITES AND SCIENCE

Meteorites are important to science because they provide a lot of information about asteroids, planets, and the formation of the solar system. Some meteorites have come from rocky objects that formed early in the history of the solar system. Many meteorites contain pieces of material that are billions of years old. For example, the Allende meteorite, which fell in Mexico in 1969, contains material that is 4.567 billion years old. This is older than Earth itself! The Murchison meteorite of Australia contains

METEORITE CLASSIFICATION

When scientists receive a new meteorite, it gets classified, meaning that it is sorted into a category. There are two systems of classification. The most popular is the Traditional Classification. In recent years, a new system called Differentiation Classification has grown in usage. Meteorite classifications are highly detailed. This section will explain the basics, and there is more information in the appendix that will help clarify the type of each meteorite described on the state pages that follow.

Traditional Meteorite Classification

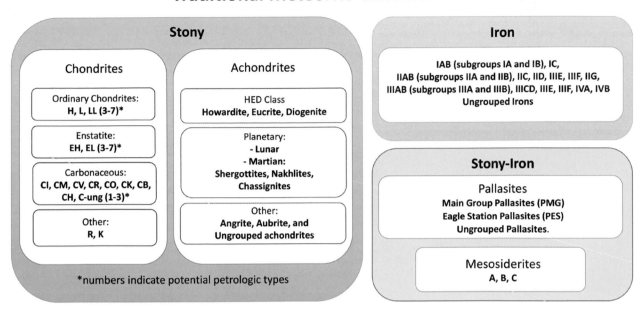

Stony

Chondrites

Ordinary Chondrites:
H, L, LL (3-7)*

Enstatite:
EH, EL (3-7)*

Carbonaceous:
CI, CM, CV, CR, CO, CK, CB, CH, C-ung (1-3)*

Other:
R, K

Achondrites

HED Class
Howardite, Eucrite, Diogenite

Planetary:
- Lunar
- Martian:
Shergottites, Nakhlites, Chassignites

Other:
Angrite, Aubrite, and Ungrouped achondrites

*numbers indicate potential petrologic types

Iron

IAB (subgroups IA and IB), IC, IIAB (subgroups IIA and IIB), IIC, IID, IIIE, IIIF, IIG, IIIAB (subgroups IIIA and IIIB), IIICD, IIIE, IIIF, IVA, IVB
Ungrouped Irons

Stony-Iron

Pallasites
Main Group Pallasites (PMG)
Eagle Station Pallasites (PES)
Ungrouped Pallasites.

Mesosiderites
A, B, C

TRADITIONAL CLASSIFICATION

Traditional classification sorts meteorites into the categories of Stony, Iron, and Stony-Iron meteorites.

STONY METEORITES

Stony meteorites are the most common category, accounting for up about 97 percent of all meteorites. They are made up of mostly silicon-based minerals, along with some iron-nickel and a few other elements. Most often, they look like a chunk of rock, as opposed to a piece of metal. Traditionally, they are divided into the **chondrites** and the **achondrites**.

Chondrites are the most common type of meteorite, accounting for about 90 percent of all documented meteorites. Chondrites contain tiny spheres called chondrules, which are particles of rock that were floating in space. Chondrites form when these particles come together and fuse into meteoroids and asteroids.

Achondrites do not contain chondrules, because these meteorites were part of asteroids or planets big enough to generate their own heat and melt rock (a process called differentiation). Lunar and Martian meteorites are examples of this type. Achondrites are rare and make up approximately 7 percent of all meteorites.

Chondrite and achondrite "groups" indicate that the meteorites are from specific asteroid sources. For example, the HED (howardite-eucrite-diogenite) group of achondrites is believed to be from the asteroid 4 Vesta.

IRON METEORITES

Iron meteorites are the classic metal objects many people imagine when they hear the word *meteorite*, but only about 2 percent of all meteorites are iron meteorites. They are made up of a mix of mostly iron, along with some nickel, and probably come from the cores of ancient asteroids. Iron meteorites can be carefully etched with certain acids to reveal metallic lines called a Widmanstätten pattern. Iron meteorites used to be classified by their Widmanstätten pattern, but they are now grouped by their chemistry, which indicates different asteroid sources.

STONY-IRON METEORITES

Stony-iron meteorites are so named because they are about half meteoritic iron-nickel and half rocky or silicate minerals. They are the rarest type, accounting for less than 1 percent of all meteorites. They are divided into two groups: **pallasites** and **mesosiderites**. Pallasites are named after the German naturalist Peter Pallas, who had studied a specimen in 1772 that contained crystals of olivine. Mesosiderites are similar to pallasites but are more of a jumbled mix of rock and metal.

DIFFERENTIATED CLASSIFICATION

Another way to look at meteorite classification is whether they are differentiated or not. *Differentiated* means that they were part of asteroids or planets big enough to generate heat and have an igneous process that melted and recrystallized the rocks. Under this classification scheme are the following categories:

UNDIFFERENTIATED

This category includes all the ordinary chondrites, the carbonaceous chondrites, the enstatites, and others.

PRIMITIVE ACHONDRITES

This category contains the achondrites that are related to the chondrites, including acapulcoites, lodranites, winonaites, and others. Surprisingly, some iron meteorites are also considered primitive achondrites because they contain inclusions indicating they were from the same source as other meteorites of this group.

DIFFERENTIATED METEORITES

This category encompasses all the meteorites from differentiated bodies. This includes all the various asteroid-sourced meteorites, such as the HED group, angrites, aubrites, ureilites, and brachinities. This category also contains most of the iron meteorites, all the stony-irons, and the lunar and Martian meteorites.

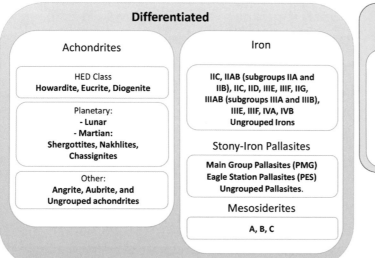

PETROLOGIC TYPE

Many chondrite meteorites are given a number, showing their petrologic type (study of the meteorite's characteristics.) Examples include H4, LL6, R3, etc.
While there are many characteristics involved, the following is a good summary:

1	2	3	4	5	6	7
Chondrules absent. Altered by water.	Chondrules present. Altered by water.	Many Pristine Chondrules	Abundant Distinct Chondrules. Slight melt.	Less Distinct Chondrules. More melted.	Indistinct Chondrules. A lot of melt.	Very melted, poorly defined chondrules.

SIDE NOTE:

Research in the field of meteorites is ongoing, and new classification techniques are being devised and new groups of meteorites are being determined.

OTHER THINGS TO KNOW ABOUT METEORITES

THERE IS MUCH MORE TO KNOW ABOUT METEORITES THAN CAN BE WRITTEN IN THIS BOOK. YOU CAN DO YOUR OWN RESEARCH TO LEARN MORE, BUT HERE ARE A FEW THINGS THAT WILL COME IN HANDY AS YOU READ:

WIDMANSTÄTTEN PATTERN

Iron and stony-iron meteorites originated in the molten cores of large asteroids. The hot cores usually contained two alloys of iron-nickel: taenite and kamacite. When the alloys cooled slowly, they formed crystals of iron-nickel. When iron and stony-iron meteorites are cut and carefully etched with certain acids, the growths of these crystals are revealed as bands of taenite and kamacite. These bands form patterns and lattices called a Widmanstätten pattern. Different meteorite groups have Widmanstätten patterns of different thicknesses.

STREWN FIELD

Sometimes a meteorite survives Earth's atmosphere and lands as a single stone. But often, larger fireballs explode or disintegrate while still many miles up in the atmosphere. When that happens, smaller fragments from the fireball land along an oval-shaped path called a strewn field. These strewn fields can be many miles long. Often, the largest meteorite will be found close to the tip of the strewn field.

CRATER

Although many people associate meteorites with craters, in fact, it is rare for a meteorite to form a crater. Almost all meteors will just plop into the earth where they land, sometimes making only a shallow hole. Only very large asteroids will hit the ground with enough energy to create a crater. It is more common for geologists to find ancient craters from impacts that happened thousands or millions of years ago.

METRIC

Meteorite collectors and meteorite researchers use the metric system of measurement when talking about meteorites. It is typical for meteorite weights to be in grams or kilograms.

Widmanstätten pattern in an iron meteorite

A strewn field map of the Homestead meteorite fall, with larger dots representing larger meteorite pieces

MAIN MASS

The largest piece of a meteorite from a fall or a find is called the main mass. Sometimes a single meteorite is cut into smaller pieces, and the largest remaining piece is the main mass.

Meteor Crater, Arizona

HAMMERS

When a meteorite hits a human-made object such as a car or a house, it is called a hammer by meteorite collectors.

THIN SECTIONS

Often scientists will mount a small piece of meteorite to a microscope slide and polish the meteorite until it is very thin, creating what's called a thin section. A lot of scientific information can be found by looking at thin sections, using special lenses in a microscope. A few meteorite examples in this book will show thin sections.

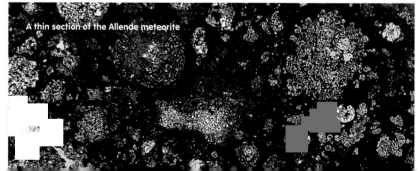

A thin section of the Allende meteorite

WHAT ARE STATE SYMBOLS?

STATES DESIGNATE OFFICIAL SYMBOLS TO RECOGNIZE AND CELEBRATE IMPORTANT CULTURAL AND NATURAL OBJECTS OF THAT STATE. SOME OF THE MORE COMMON STATE SYMBOLS INCLUDE STATE FLAGS AND STATE SEALS, BUT THERE ARE ALSO STATE MINERALS, STATE FOSSILS, AND STATE GEMSTONES.

Examples of state symbols: Rhodochrosite is the state mineral of Colorado. Megalodon is the state fossil of North Carolina. Texas Blue Topaz is the state gem of Texas.

THERE ARE CURRENTLY NO OFFICIAL STATE METEORITES

Currently no states have an official meteorite, even though meteorites have been found in 46 of the 50 states. However, someone—including you!—could work on getting a meteorite designated. It is up to us to get these marvels from outer space recognized in our own home states. Here's how:

HOW TO DESIGNATE A STATE METEORITE

1. A person or group decides that their state needs a state meteorite.

2. Either individually or collectively, the citizens of that state research the meteorites found within the state's boundaries and propose one to be officially designated. This is often done by classrooms of students, hobbyists, or even industry groups.

3. The individual or group contacts the elected representatives of the state and works with them to write a bill designating the state meteorite.

4. The bill goes through the legislative process and is voted on, usually by both the House of Representatives and Senate of that state.

5. If the bill makes it through the legislature and is then signed by the governor, the state meteorite is designated by law.

MAP OF THE UNITED STATES
SHOWING RANGES OF HOW MANY METEORITES HAVE BEEN FOUND

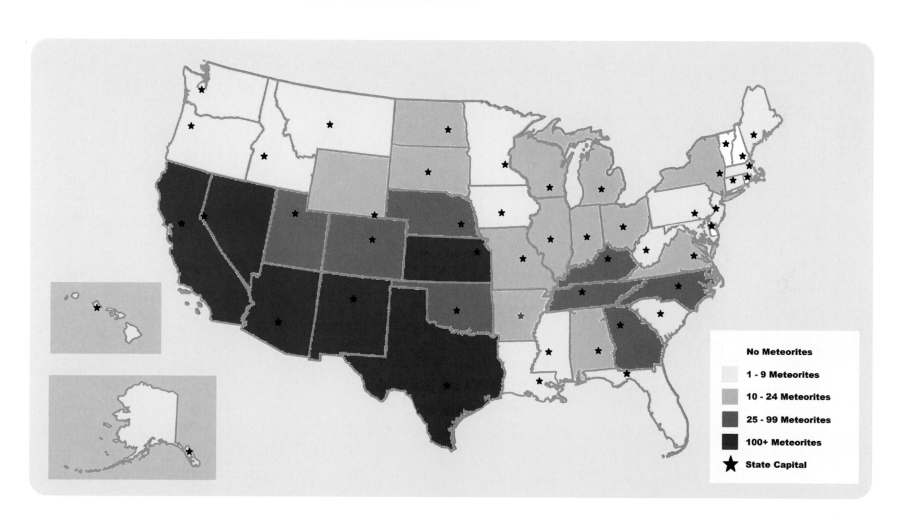

No Meteorites

1 - 9 Meteorites

10 - 24 Meteorites

25 - 99 Meteorites

100+ Meteorites

★ State Capital

Alabama

State Capital

Site of mentioned meteorite fall

Site of mentioned meteorite find

A slice of the Leighton meteorite

Total known meteorites from Alabama: 18

OTHER NOTABLE METEORITES:

Leighton: This 877-gram (1.9 lb.) H5 chondrite fell on January 12, 1907, and reportedly made a whizzing sound. The meteorite landed in the yard of Mrs. M. D. Allen, who witnessed the fall from her front porch.

Felix: On May 15, 1900, there was a meteor sighting and reportedly three stones were seen, but only one was recovered. It turned out to be a rare 3.2-kilogram (7 lb.) CO3.3 carbonaceous chondrite. Felix is the only CO3.3 found outside Africa or Antarctica.

SYLACAUGA

TYPE: H4 Chondrite
FELL: November 30, 1954
MASS: 5.56 kilograms (12.25 lbs.)

Shortly after noon on November 30, 1954, a loud noise was heard over the skies of Alabama. Soon afterward, a grapefruit-sized meteorite smashed through the roof of a house and hit Ann Elizabeth Fowler Hodges as she was napping on her sofa. Hodges ended up with a large bruise on her body, making this the first well-documented case of a meteorite injuring a person. The meteorite ended up in a lawsuit over who owned it: the Hodges family or the property owner. Eventually, the family bought the rights to the meteorite for $500. In 1956, they donated the specimen to the Alabama Museum of Natural History, where it can be seen today.

Sylacauga meteorite held by Dr. Walter B. Jones, director of the Alabama Museum of Natural History, in 1956

Total known meteorites from Alaska: 4

OTHER NOTABLE METEORITES:

Chilkoot: In 1881, the State Mining Bureau of California purchased a 43-kilogram (94 lb.) Iron IIIAB meteorite from Chief "Donawack," who said it had been witnessed as a fall about a hundred years earlier by a member of his tribe near Chilkoot Inlet.

Cold Bay: About 320 grams (0.7 lbs.) of a Pallasite PES meteorite were found in 1921. It is one of only five pallasites of the PES group in the world.

The main mass of the Aggie Creek meteorite

A slice of the Chilkoot meteorite

AGGIE CREEK

TYPE: Iron IIIAB
FOUND: 1942
MASS: 43 kilograms (94 lbs.)

On August 11, 1942, a gold-dredging operation on Aggie Creek picked up a heavy metal object from 12 feet below the Earth's surface. The dredge operator, a Mr. Dent, heard a loud bang and went to investigate. He found a heavy mass that he initially thought was a gold nugget, but it turned out to be an iron meteorite weighing 43 kilograms (94 lbs.). This specimen is tied with one other as the largest meteorite from Alaska. The biggest portion is in the collection of the University of Alaska.

Arizona

Aerial picture of Meteor Crater in Arizona

Total known meteorites from Arizona: 178

OTHER NOTABLE METEORITES:

Tucson: Two famous meteorites were first mentioned in literature in the 1850s but were known to the local Spanish Mexican population around Tucson well before then. One meteorite is ring shaped and named Irwin-Ainsa; it weighs 621 kilograms (1,367 lbs.). The other is bowl shaped and named Carleton; it weighs 282 kilograms (621 lbs.). Both are ungrouped iron meteorites and were used as anvils.

Holbrook: On July 19, 1912, a meteor exploded near the town of Aztec and showered it with over 16,000 small meteorites. Most of these L/LL6 chondrite meteorites weigh only a few grams, but some were as heavy as 6 kilograms (13 lbs.). Over 220 kilograms (484 lbs.) have been recovered.

CANYON DIABLO

TYPE: Iron IAB-MG
FOUND: 1891
MASS: 30+ tons (60,000+ lbs.)

A specimen of a Canyon Diablo meteorite

The most famous meteorite crater in the United States is Meteor Crater in Arizona, also known as Barringer Crater. About 50,000 years ago, an asteroid roughly 160 feet across impacted the site and created a crater that currently measures 3,900 feet across and 560 feet deep. Tons of meteorite fragments littered the terrain around the crater and have been used by American Indians as a source of iron. The fragments were documented as the Canyon Diablo meteorite in 1891, but the crater was not recognized as an impact crater until Daniel Barringer filed a mining claim to it and studied it for several years. The Barringer family still owns the crater, which is a popular tourist destination.

Woman posing with the Tucson Ring meteorite

Total known meteorites from Arkansas: 15

OTHER NOTABLE METEORITES:

Success: On April 18, 1924, a meteor appeared over northeastern Arkansas with a flash and the sound of rumbling thunder. A man found the 3.5-kilogram (7.7 lb.) meteorite the next morning. It passed through various people's possession until it was acquired by the Smithsonian Institution in 1973. It is an L6 chondrite.

Hope: Mistakenly thought to be from Alabama, this meteorite was found while a farmer was plowing in Hope, Arkansas, several years before it ended up in the possession of a school teacher in Alabama. It's a 6.8-kilogram (14.9 lb.) Iron IAB-MG meteorite.

The Paragould meteorite

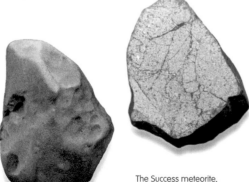

The Success meteorite, with a cut face showing the interior

In the early morning hours of February 17, 1930, a large fireball was seen over the skies of several midwestern states. The fireball split into several pieces, and the largest piece created an 8-foot-deep hole on a farm near the town of Paragould, Arkansas. The impact threw dirt and debris up to 150 feet away. The LL5 chondrite meteorite measured over 3 feet across and is the second-largest witnessed meteorite fall in the United States. It was initially sold to the Chicago Field Museum before being placed on long-term loan to the University of Arkansas.

Success

Paragould

★ Little Rock

Hope

★ State Capital

Site of mentioned meteorite fall

Site of mentioned meteorite find

PARAGOULD

TYPE: LL5 Chondrite
FELL: February 17, 1930
MASS: 408 kilograms (889 lbs.)

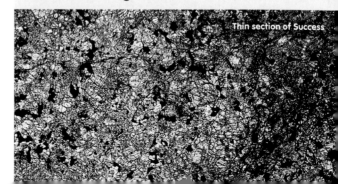

Thin section of Success

California

A specimen of Creston

Total known meteorites from California: 274

OTHER NOTABLE METEORITES:

Creston: A fireball was spotted by hundreds of people over California on the evening of October 23, 2015. Meteorite hunters figured out the fall area based on the trajectory of the fireball and Doppler radar returns. More than 688 grams (1.4 lbs.) of this L6 chondrite were recovered over the next few weeks throughout a 6-mile-long strewn field.

Sutter's Mill: On April 22, 2012, a fireball was seen moving west over Nevada and California. A sonic boom was heard near Lake Tahoe, and the meteor fragmented into small pieces. Over the next few weeks, 993 grams (2.1 lbs.) of this rare C carbonaceous chondrite were found.

Model of the Old Woman meteorite

State Capital

Site of mentioned meteorite fall

Site of mentioned meteorite find

OLD WOMAN

TYPE: Iron IIAB
FOUND: 1976
MASS: 2,753 kilograms (6,069 lbs.)

In 1976, two prospectors searching for a lost gold mine in the Old Woman Mountains of California found what turned out to be the second-largest iron meteorite known in the United States. Because the land was owned by the US government, the men tried to file a mining claim so that they could claim ownership of the meteorite. The government countered that meteorites do not count as a valuable mineral deposit according to federal mining laws. The meteorite was airlifted out of the mountains by the Marines and eventually made its way to the Smithsonian for study and display. Over the next few years, multiple lawsuits were filed over ownership of the meteorite, but they were unsuccessful. The main mass of the Old Woman meteorite is now on display at the Desert Discovery Center in Barstow, California.

Total known meteorites from Colorado: **90**

OTHER NOTABLE METEORITES:

Elbert: On January 11, 1998, a fireball was reported over Elbert County, Colorado. Two years later, five-year-old Dustin Riffel was picking up rocks near his house with his mother and found a black rock that turned out to be a 681-gram (1.49 lb.) meteorite from the fall. Several other stones of this LL6 chondrite were eventually found as well.

Guffey: In 1907, two cowboys were riding after cattle when they came upon a 309-kilogram (680 lb.) iron mass. It turned out to be an ungrouped iron meteorite and is the biggest meteorite found in Colorado to date.

A specimen of the Johnstown meteorite, showing the interior

Johnstown
★ Denver
Elbert
Guffey

★ State Capital
Site of mentioned meteorite fall
Site of mentioned meteorite find

The main mass of the Elbert meteorite

JOHNSTOWN

TYPE: Diogenite
FELL: July 6, 1924
MASS: 40.3 kilograms (88.8 lbs.)

The fall of the Johnstown meteorite interrupted a funeral, with loud crackling sounds in the sky heard just before a 6.8-kilogram (15 lb.) meteorite hit the ground near the church, creating a hole almost 2 feet deep. Over the next few days, several other stones were recovered throughout the area. The largest stone weighted 23.5 kilograms (51 lbs.). After the stone was studied, it was found to be a diogenite with a lovely olive-green interior. Diogenites are a member of the HED (howardite-eucrite-diogenite) group of achondrite meteorites.

Connecticut

★ Hartford

Weathersfield

Weston

★ State Capital

Site of mentioned meteorite fall

Site of mentioned meteorite find

A large portion of the Weston meteorite

WESTON

TYPE: H4 Chondrite
FELL: December 14, 1807
MASS: 150 kilograms (330 lbs.)

A large meteorite fall occurred on the morning of December 14, 1807, becoming the first well-documented and published fall in a scientific journal in the United States. Quickly after the fall, two Yale professors, Benjamin Silliman and James Kingsley, went to the area and thoroughly documented the locations and details of each major piece of the meteorite. The largest weighed 90.7 kilograms (200 lbs.) and tore a gash 5 feet long and 3 feet deep into the ground, throwing debris up to 100 feet away. The professors published their study in 1809 and provided such great detail that, a century later, researchers were able to map a 9-mile-long strewn field of the area.

Total known meteorites from Connecticut: 5

OTHER NOTABLE METEORITES:

Wethersfield (1971) and Wethersfield (1982):
In a remarkable occurrence, the town of Wethersfield has had two meteorites fall only eleven years apart, and distance-wise only 2 miles apart. On April 8, 1971, a meteorite smashed through the roof of Mr. and Mrs. Cassarino's house and was found in the morning partially embedded in the ceiling. It was a 350-gram (0.77 lb.) L6 chondrite. Eleven years later, a meteorite fell on November 8, 1982, traveling through the roof of a house belonging to Mr. and Mrs. Donahue. The main mass of 2,760 grams (5.9 lbs.) also turned out to be an L6 chondrite.

Specimen of Wethersfield (1982)

METEOR-WRONG: VENTIFACTS

A meteor-wrong is an unofficial term for a rock that looks like a meteorite but is not. One common meteor-wrong are ventifacts: rocks that have been ablated by wind-driven sand or ice. These rocks will often have an aerodynamic and polished look that makes them look similar to meteorites, but they are not.

Example of a ventifact

Dover

★ State Capital

⚡ Site of mentioned meteorite fall

🪨 Site of mentioned meteorite find

Landscape of some rural parts of Delaware

NO METEORITES HAVE BEEN FOUND IN DELAWARE

Delaware is the second-smallest state by land area, with 1,982 square miles of land ranging from forest to farmland to urban areas and beaches. Some meteors have been sighted over Delaware, but because much of the state is on the coast, any potential meteorites likely ended up in the ocean. East Coast states usually experience more humidity and rain as well, which means that meteorites will quickly weather and deteriorate. That's why it would be rare for an old meteorite to be discovered in this area. The best way to find a meteorite in Delaware would be to wait for a fresh fall or to search old rock walls and farm fields (with the owner's permission, of course).

Florida

State Capital
Site of mentioned meteorite fall
Site of mentioned meteorite find

Total known meteorites from Florida: 6

A 75-gram Osceola lying in sand where it was found

OTHER NOTABLE METEORITES:

Grayton: An 11.3-kilogram (24.8 lb.) H5 chondrite was found on a local beach in 1983. Two people with metal detectors uncovered it between sand dunes, buried 3 feet among potsherds. The location suggests that it was part of a discard pile and may have been transported there by American Indians.

Orlando: On November 8, 2004, Donna Shuford heard an object hit the side of her house. Apparently, a 180-gram (0.4 lb.) eucrite meteorite had fallen on her car and bounced off, striking her house.

OSCEOLA

TYPE: L6 Chondrite
FELL: January 24, 2016
MASS: 1,099 grams+ (2.42 lbs.)

On the morning of Sunday, January 24, 2016, a fireball was seen in the skies over northern Florida. Witnesses described a sparkling object leaving a white smoke plume in its wake. Researchers managed to get weather radar data from that time and used it to track where the meteorite may have landed. The first fragment of the meteorite, weighing 8.5 grams (0.018 lbs.), was found six days after the event. The largest piece, embedded in sandy ground, weighed 839 grams (1.84 lbs.).

A cleaned-up Osceola meteorite

A sliced piece of the Grayton meteorite

Total known meteorites from Georgia: 27

OTHER NOTABLE METEORITES:

Losttown: A 3-kilogram (6.6 lb.) meteorite was plowed up on a farm in 1867. It was quickly purchased by meteorite researchers and was eventually found to be an Iron IID meteorite with a great Widmanstätten pattern.

Forsyth: Georgia's first meteorite fall occurred on May 8, 1829. A dark cloud followed by two explosions occurred near the town of Forsyth, and a 16.3-kilogram (35.9 lb.) meteorite was found shortly after. It turned out to be an L6 chondrite.

The back plate of the mailbox struck by the Claxton meteorite

State Capital

Site of mentioned meteorite fall

Site of mentioned meteorite find

An etched section of the Losttown meteorite

A slice of the Claxton meteorite

CLAXTON

TYPE: L6 Chondrite
FELL: December 10, 1984
MASS: 1,455 grams (3.18 lbs.)

Meteorites that hit human-made objects are called hammers, and on December 10, 1984, one struck a mailbox. People nearby heard a whistling sound just before a crash as the meteorite crushed and knocked down a mailbox before embedding itself in the ground. The family who owned the land sold the meteorite for $3,000 and the mailbox for $1,500. The mailbox was resold at an auction in 2007 for $83,000, making it possibly one of the most expensive mailboxes in the world.

Hawaii

Total known meteorites from Hawaii: 2

Palolo Valley: On April 24, 1949, a meteorite landed in the Territory of Hawaii and is the only other meteorite from this state. It tore a hole in the eave of a house and buried itself in the lawn. The damage, and its cause, was discovered the next morning. It was a 682-gram (1.5 lb.) H5 chondrite. Most of the meteorite was placed with the geology department of the University of Hawaii, but unfortunately it appears to have been lost in the 1970s.

Palolo Valley

Honolulu

★ State Capital

Site of mentioned meteorite fall

Site of mentioned meteorite find

A specimen of the Honolulu meteorite

HONOLULU

TYPE: L5 Chondrite
FELL: September 27, 1825
MASS: 2.42+ kilograms (5.3+ lbs.)

During the era of the Kingdom of Hawaii, long before it became a US state, a large meteorite disintegrated over several of the islands on the morning of September 27, 1825. Pieces of the meteorite were gathered by the Indigenous peoples, as well as by visiting sailors who brought the specimens to museums around the world. The official total weight is 2.42 kilograms (5.3 lbs.), but it is likely that many more meteorites were found and never documented, possibly still sitting around in family collections.

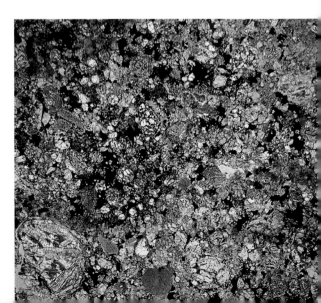

Thin section of Palolo valley

Thin section of Honolulu

Total known meteorites from Idaho: 8

OTHER NOTABLE METEORITES:

Oakley (iron): In 1926, two children were fixing fences, and as one of them dragged an axe, it hit something on the ground and made a clanging sound. It turned out to be a 111-kilogram (244 lb) Iron IIIF meteorite and is the largest meteorite from Idaho. Not to be confused with Oakley (stone), which is a H6 chondrite from Kansas.

Jerome: This 6.8-kilogram (15 lb.) L chondrite meteorite was found in 1954. It is classified as an L chondrite because no one has bothered conducting additional classification work for it.

The Jerome meteorite

A slice of the Wilder meteorite

State Capital

Site of mentioned meteorite fall

Site of mentioned meteorite find

The Oakley (iron) meteorite

WILDER

TYPE: H5 Chondrite
FOUND: 1982
MASS: 28.5 kilograms (62 lbs.)

In 1982, Alan Noe found an odd rock in an unplowed field north of the town of Wilder, Idaho. In 1987, he took the 1,970-gram (4.3 lb.) rock to Boise State University, where it was identified as a chondritic meteorite. In 1990, a second piece of the same meteorite was found a short distance from the first one, but this piece weighed 26.6 kilograms (58 lbs.). The meteorite has a very weathered surface, which indicates that it has been on Earth for a while, and a dark interior.

Illinois

Park Forest

Saint Augustine

★ Springfield

Benld

★ State Capital

Site of mentioned meteorite fall

Site of mentioned meteorite find

A specimen of a Park Forest meteorite, with some yellow paint from when it hit a fire plug

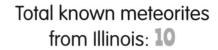

Total known meteorites from Illinois: 10

OTHER NOTABLE METEORITES:

Saint Augustine: A 22-kilogram (48.4 lb.) iron IID meteorite was found in 1974 by a person digging fence-post holes.

Benld: A 1.7-kilogram (3.9 lb.) H6 chondrite meteorite hit a parked car in a garage on September 29, 1938. The meteorite tore through both the wooden garage roof and the car roof. Parts of the car and meteorite were on display at the Field Museum in Chicago.

A slice of the Benld meteorite

PARK FOREST

TYPE: L5 Chondrite
FELL: March 26, 2003
MASS: 18+ kilograms (39+ lbs.)

Just before midnight on March 26, 2003, a fireball lit up the skies over several midwestern states, and the village of Park Forest, just south of Chicago, was pelted with fresh meteorites. Hundreds of small stone meteorites landed on rooftops, yards, and streets throughout the area, damaging windows and roofs. The largest piece weighed over 5.26 kilograms (11.5 lbs.). Meteorite hunters and locals scoured the area for days, finding many additional specimens.

Thin section of Park Forest

Total known meteorites from Indiana: 13

OTHER NOTABLE METEORITES:

Hamlet: On the evening of October 13, 1959, a meteorite hit the rain gutter of a house and bounced off. The homeowners, Mr. and Mrs. Hall, came out and found a 2-kilogram (4.4 lb.) meteorite lying in the street. It turned out to be an LL4 chondrite. Surprisingly, a second meteorite from the fall was found four years later by the Halls' son.

Williams: A 1-kilogram (2.2 lb.) H4 chondrite meteorite was found by Douglas May while tilling his garden in 2012.

The Lafayette meteorite

State Capital
Site of mentioned meteorite fall
Site of mentioned meteorite find

A specimen of Hamlet

In 1931, a Dr. Farrington found an 800-gram (1.76 lb.) rock in a drawer in Purdue University's geological collection and recognized it as a meteorite. The story behind how it ended up in the drawer is murky, but lore says that a student saw the meteorite fall on the edge of a pond, and brought it to the university, where it was misidentified as a glacial rock and put in the drawer. In 1976, the Viking spaceship landed on Mars and gathered information on that planet's atmosphere. Comparing that data with the chemistry of the Lafayette meteorite showed that the meteorite originally came from Mars. Some time ago, a large asteroid had hit Mars and knocked pieces of the planet into space. Some of those pieces eventually fell to Earth as Martian meteorites.

LAFAYETTE

TYPE: Nakhlite—Martian Meteorite
FOUND: 1931
MASS: 800 grams (1.76 lbs.)

Top view of Lafayette meteorite

Iowa

Estherville

Marion

Homestead

★ Des Moines

★ State Capital

Site of mentioned meteorite fall

Site of mentioned meteorite find

A sliced portion of the Homestead meteorite

Total known meteorites from Iowa: 7

OTHER NOTABLE METEORITES:

Marion (Iowa): Iowa's first meteorite fall occurred on February 25, 1847. Witnesses reported hearing a rushing sound, followed by an explosion. The fall consisted of 28 kilograms (61 lbs.) of fragments of this L6 chondrite.

Estherville: A mesosiderite A3/4 meteorite fell on May 10, 1879. More than 320 kilograms (700 lbs.) of this metallic meteorite showered a 7-mile path north of the town of Estherville. When people realized that it was valuable, a meteorite rush started, with locals hunting for fragments to sell to traders.

HOMESTEAD

TYPE: L5 Chondrite
FELL: February 12, 1875
MASS: 230 kilograms (510 lbs.)

Close-up of Estherville meteorite

A blazing fireball was seen over the Midwest on the evening of February 12, 1875. It was described as a brilliant light with a long tail throwing out red sparks and jets of purple flames. It exploded over eastern Iowa, and several hundred pounds of meteorite fragments fell over the countryside. The first meteorite was found three days later, but most were not discovered until the snow had melted two months later. Of the more than one hundred found specimens, the largest fragment weighed 34 kilograms (74 lbs.) and was buried 2 feet deep. The meteorite turned out to be an L5 chondrite, and because there were so many specimens, it has been distributed to museums around the world.

A slice of an Estherville meteorite

Total known meteorites from Kansas: 147

OTHER NOTABLE METEORITES:

Norton County: Over 1.1 tons (2,200 lbs.) of this rare aubrite meteorite fell on February 18, 1948, in Norton County, Kansas, and Furnas County, Nebraska. One of only 75 known aubrite meteorites, it has a fragmented lightcolored interior composed of ortho-pyroxene crystals and enstatite. The largest piece weighed 2,200 pounds and blasted a hole 6 feet wide and 6 feet deep. This is the largest witnessed fall in the United States.

Admire: This meteorite was found in 1881, and it had green olivine crystals in metal. So far, over 180 kilograms (396 lbs.) of this Pallasite PMG meteorite have been found.

A cleaned nugget of the Admire meteorite with olivine crystals

A peridot gemstone faceted from the olivine from Admire meteorite

A slice of the Brenham meteorite, backlit to show the olivine crystals

State Capital

Site of mentioned meteorite fall

Site of mentioned meteorite find

BRENHAM

TYPE: Pallasite PMG-an
FOUND: 1882
MASS: 4.3+ tons (8,500+ lbs.)

Although the Brenham meteorite was officially discovered in 1882, pieces of it had been used in tools and crafts by Indigenous cultures long before then. Beads made from the Brenham meteorite have been found over 1,000 miles away in Hopewell culture sites in Ohio. The meteorite itself is associated with a small crater called Haviland Crater, and several tons of pallasite meteorite have been dug up. The meteorite features yellow-green crystals of olivine among iron-nickel, making for an attractive specimen when sliced. There are thousands of fragments of Brenham, with the largest found in 2005. It weighed 650 kilograms (1,430 lbs.).

A chunk of Norton County aubrite

Kentucky

Total known meteorites from Kentucky: 25

OTHER NOTABLE METEORITES:

Cumberland Falls: This 17-kilogram (37 lb.) aubrite meteorite fell on April 9, 1919. The meteor was tracked and documented by telegraph operators as it traveled through the skies of the region.

Eagle Station: This 36-kilogram (79 lb.) pallasite meteorite was found in 1880. It turned out to have a slightly different chemistry from other pallasites, resulting in the designation of a new group of pallasites known as PES—Pallasite Eagle Station.

Eagle Station

★ Frankfort

Cumberland Falls

Murray

★ State Capital

Site of mentioned meteorite fall

Site of mentioned meteorite find

A slice of the Murray carbonaceous chondrite

MURRAY

TYPE: CM2 Carbonaceous Chondrite
FELL: September 20, 1950
MASS: 12.6 kilograms (27.7 lbs.)

A bright meteor exploded over Kentucky on September 20, 1950. A month later, a search conducted by Vanderbilt University found several meteorites, with the largest weighing 3.5 kilograms (7.7 lbs.). Several homes were apparently also hit by the meteorite, though the owners didn't make an issue of it. The specimens turned out to be from a CM2 carbonaceous meteorite. CM and CM2 meteorites are special because some contain complex chemical compounds such as amino acids. Murray was eventually found to have 17 different amino acids, adding to our understanding of the early solar system.

A fragment of the Cumberland Falls aubrite

Another view of Cumberland Falls

Total known meteorites from Louisiana: 3

OTHER NOTABLE METEORITES:

Atlanta: This 5.5-kilogram (12 lb.) EL6 chondrite meteorite was found in 1938.

Greenwell Springs: A 664-gram (1.46 lb.) LL4 chondrite meteorite was found by a homeowner in his front yard on November 30, 1987. It is suspected that the meteorite had fallen sometime in the previous week.

A piece of the New Orleans meteorite

Atlanta

Greenwell Springs

★ Baton Rouge

New Orleans

★ State Capital

Site of mentioned meteorite fall

Site of mentioned meteorite find

Another fragment of the New Orleans meteorite

A slice of Greenwell Springs

NEW ORLEANS

TYPE: H5 Chondrite
FELL: September 23, 2003
MASS: 19.26 kilograms (42 lbs.)

A meteorite hit a New Orleans house on the afternoon of September 23, 2003. No one was home at the time, but the owner returned later to find a lot of damage, including a hole in the roof and in each floor. A meteorite had smashed all the way into the crawlspace, leaving fragments and debris along the way. The largest piece weighed 2,966 grams (6.53 lbs.). The homeowner took the fragments to a local university, where it was confirmed to be a meteorite.

Maine

State Capital
Site of mentioned meteorite fall
Site of mentioned meteorite find

Total known meteorites from Maine: 5

A fragment of Nobleborough

OTHER NOTABLE METEORITES:

Searsmont: A 5.4-kilogram (11.8 lb.) meteorite fell on May 21, 1871, becoming the third meteorite to fall in Maine. It reportedly sounded like a heavy gun blast and is an H5 chondrite.

Andover: A 3.2-kilogram (7 lb.) L6 chondrite fell on August 5, 1898. It was the fourth documented meteorite to fall in Maine and was reported to sound like a buzz saw as it fell.

NOBLEBOROUGH

TYPE: Eucrite
FELL: August 7, 1823
MASS: 2.3 kilograms (5 lbs.)

On August 7, 1823, a Mr. Dinsmore heard what sounded like a platoon of soldiers firing guns. He saw a white cloud spiraling toward him, and a stone struck the ground within 100 feet, frightening away some sheep. He dug up the stone, which turned out to be the first meteorite found in the state of Maine. Specimens were highly sought after by curators and collectors, and little of this meteorite remains today.

A slice of Andover

Total known meteorites from Maryland: 4

OTHER NOTABLE METEORITES:

Emmitsburg: The origin of this meteorite is murky. It is said that a 450-gram (1 lb.) mass was found in Emmitsburg in 1854; it entered the collection of Dr. Chilton of New York before being further divided and distributed among other collections. It is likely an Iron IIIAB, but that designation could be an error since pieces were mixed up with other iron meteorites.

St. Mary's County: A meteor exploded over St. Mary's County on June 20, 1919. A retired sea captain named John Forrest saw it explode, and a piece landed 20 feet in front of him. He placed the meteorite on a shelf. Years later, his grandson took a sample to be analyzed, and in 1969 it was classified as an LL3.3 chondrite. The larger piece found by the captain was lost; only 24.3 grams (0.05 lbs.) remain.

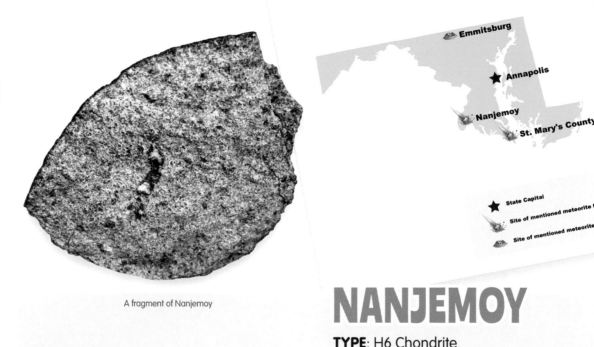

A fragment of Nanjemoy

NANJEMOY

TYPE: H6 Chondrite
FELL: February 10, 1825
MASS: 7.5 kilograms (16.5 lbs.)

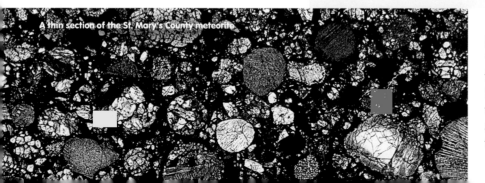

A thin section of the St. Mary's County meteorite

Maryland's first documented meteorite fall occurred on February 10, 1825. It exploded with what was reported to sound like cannon fire, followed by a loud buzzing noise. The single stone buried itself 24 inches under the earth's surface and threw mud up to 30 feet away. It was initially thought to be a stone blasted from a quarry several miles away. The meteorite weighed 7.5 kilograms (16.5 lbs.) and turned out to be an H6 chondrite.

(map labels)
Emmitsburg
Annapolis
Nanjemoy
St. Mary's County
State Capital
Site of mentioned meteorite fall
Site of mentioned meteorite find

Massachusetts

- ★ State Capital
- Site of mentioned meteorite fall
- Site of mentioned meteorite find

Total known meteorites from Massachusetts: 2

Northampton: The only other official meteorite from Massachusetts is a 353-gram (0.77 lb.) iron meteorite that was found in 1963.

A cut section of the Northampton meteorite

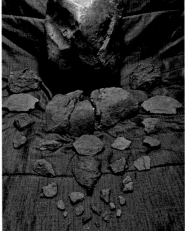

The Barnstable meteorite

BARNSTABLE

TYPE: H4 Chondrite
FOUND: 2018
MASS: 14.28 kilograms (31.4 lbs.)

On August 18, 2018, a meteorite hunter named Stephen J. Amara Jr. of Massachusetts set out on a hike with his family. On the way, he found a few rocks and took them home. Two weeks later, he examined one and found that it had all the indications of being a meteorite. He sent a sample for testing and went back into the woods to find more. He eventually dug out the main mass, which weighed 10.8 kilograms (24 lbs). It turned out to be an H4 chondrite and was officially accepted as a meteorite on January 23, 2019.

The main mass of the Barnstable meteorite right after it was discovered and uncovered

Total known meteorites from Michigan: 12

A cut and etched portion of Rose City

OTHER NOTABLE METEORITES:

Rose City: A meteor was spotted over Michigan on October 17, 1921. The next day, a meteorite was found on the farm of George Hall, with two others found soon after. There was a total weight of 10.6 kilograms (23 lbs.), and it is an H5 chondrite.

Hamburg: Hundreds of people across several states witnessed a meteor in the sky on the evening of January 18, 2018; it fell over an area near the town of Hamburg. Eventually more than 1,000 grams (2.2 lbs.) of this H4 chondrite were recovered by meteorite hunters.

Another view of Rose City

Rose City

Lansing

Worden

Hamburg

★ State Capital

Site of mentioned meteorite fall

Site of mentioned meteorite find

The Worden meteorite

WORDEN

TYPE: L5 Chondrite
FELL: September 1, 1997
MASS: 1,551 grams (4.3 lbs.)

The car that was dented by the Worden meteorite

On the late afternoon of September 1, 1997, many people saw a bright meteor over central and southern Michigan. It was extremely bright and broke up into multiple pieces before one crashed into a garage and dented a car parked inside. This meteorite turned out to be a 1.55-kilogram (4.3 lb.) L5 chondrite, and it still carries red paint chips from where it dented the car.

Minnesota

A cut and etched specimen of Arlington

Total known meteorites from Minnesota: 9

OTHER NOTABLE METEORITES:

Euclid: This 2.5-kilogram (5.5 lb.) H5 chondrite was found in a field in 1970. It was kept in a coffee can for 26 years before being brought to researchers.

Arlington: This 8.94-kilogram (19 lb.) iron IIE-an meteorite was found in 1894, the same year as the Fisher fall.

A slice of the Fisher meteorite

FISHER

TYPE: L6 Chondrite
FELL: April 9, 1894
MASS: 17.6 kilograms (38 lbs.)

Loud detonations were heard on April 9, 1894, over western Minnesota, but it wasn't until summer that two meteorites were found. One weighed 4.2 kilograms (9.2 lbs.). The other was originally larger but had been broken into smaller pieces. Several other stones were found in the next few years. This was the first and only documented meteorite fall in Minnesota and is an L6 chondrite.

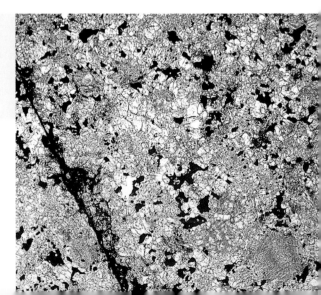

Thin section of the Fisher meteorite

Total known meteorites from Mississippi: 4

OTHER NOTABLE METEORITES:

Palahatchie: A meteor was spotted on the morning of October 17, 1910, witnessed by thousands of people near the town of Pelahatchie. The meteor exploded and showered fragments over the area. All the fragments were small, with the largest weighing 2 pounds. The last classification of this meteorite is OC (ordinary chondrite), because most of its specimens have been lost and not been properly reclassified.

Tupelo: A 280-gram (0.6 lb.) EL6 enstatite chondrite was found by people looking for artifacts in a plowed field at a family farm.

Samples of the Baldwyn meteorite

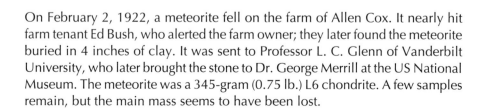

The Baldwyn meteorite

Fragments of the Palahatchie meteorite

BALDWYN

TYPE: L6 Chondrite
FELL: 1922
MASS: 345 grams (0.75 lbs.)

On February 2, 1922, a meteorite fell on the farm of Allen Cox. It nearly hit farm tenant Ed Bush, who alerted the farm owner; they later found the meteorite buried in 4 inches of clay. It was sent to Professor L. C. Glenn of Vanderbilt University, who later brought the stone to Dr. George Merrill at the US National Museum. The meteorite was a 345-gram (0.75 lb.) L6 chondrite. A few samples remain, but the main mass seems to have been lost.

Missouri

A small slice of the
Faucett meteorite

State Capital

Site of mentioned meteorite fall

Site of mentioned meteorite find

Total known meteorites from Missouri: 24

OTHER NOTABLE METEORITES:

St. Louis: This 1-kilogram (2.2 lb.) H4 chondrite meteorite fell on December 10, 1950, hitting a moving car driven by John Houser. It ripped through the top of his convertible, and he initially thought he had blown a tire.

Faucett: In the summer of 1907, a farmer named E. W. Spencer saw a spectacular meteor in the sky that appeared to fall near his land. In April 1966, the farmer's son found a 12-pound rock in a plowed field, which turned out to be a meteorite. Numerous fragments of this meteorite were found over the next few years, weighing more than 100 kilograms (220 lbs.) in total. The meteorite is fairly weathered H5 chondrite, which suggests that it predates the meteor sighted by Spencer in 1907.

CONCEPTION JUNCTION

TYPE: Pallasite PMG-an
FOUND: 2006
MASS: 17 kilograms (37 lbs.)

In 2006, a farmer noticed an odd hunk of metal protruding from a hillside and dug it out. He sawed off one end and found yellow-green crystals embedded in the metal, suggesting that it was a meteorite. In 2009, meteorite hunters heard about the find and purchased it from the farmer. It was analyzed and found to be a pallasite of the PMG-an group. The meteorite was officially classified and in 2011 was named Conception Junction. It is one of two pallasites from Missouri.

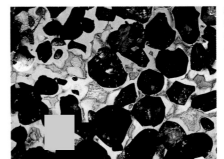

A close-up of the olivine crystals in metal of Conception Junction

A slice of Conception Junction featuring olivine crystals

Total known meteorites from Montana: 7

OTHER NOTABLE METEORITES:

Roundup: A family had been using an unusually heavy 17.5-kilogram (38.5 lb.) rock as a doorstop at their ranch for years before having the specimen analyzed in 1990. It turned out to be an Iron IIIAB meteorite.

Choteau: A potential meteorite was purchased at an estate sale of a Choteau resident in 2011, and it turned out to be a pallasite, ungrouped, and weighed 8.47 kilograms (18.6 lbs.). It is likely to have been found locally by the resident.

A slice of Twodot

★ State Capital

Site of mentioned meteorite fall

Site of mentioned meteorite find

A slice of Choteau

Close-up of the olivine crystals in the Choteau meteorite

TWODOT

TYPE: H6 Chondrite
FOUND: 1999
MASS: 21.4 kilograms (47 lbs.)

In many other states, there are a lot of chondrite meteorites, but Twodot is the only chondrite out of seven meteorites found in Montana. It was found by a hunter who came upon a rock with an unusual shape while hunting for elk. Even though the hunter had no experience with meteorite hunting, the oriented rock made him think that it might be a meteorite. Years later it was officially confirmed to be a 21.4-kilogram (47 lb.) H6 chondrite.

Nebraska

A fragment of the Sioux County meteorite

* State Capital
* Site of mentioned meteorite fall
* Site of mentioned meteorite find

A slice of the Owasco meteorite

Total known meteorites from Nebraska: **50**

OTHER NOTABLE METEORITES:

Owasco: This 168.4-kilogram (370 lb.) L6 chondrite was found by a farmer in a field in 1984. Astoundingly, a 6.69-kilogram (14.7 lb.) L6 chondrite called Oliver was also found in the same field that year. The two have different levels of weathering, suggesting that they are from different old falls.

Bayard: A 75-kilogram (165 lb.) L5 chondrite meteorite was discovered by Dr. Art Struempler while he was sorting through a junk pile on his family's farm in 1982. It is shaped like a large football.

SIOUX COUNTY

TYPE: Eucrite
FELL: August 8, 1933
MASS: 4.1 kilograms (9 lbs.)

A large meteor fell through the skies of Nebraska on August 8, 1933, with what was described as a long plume of white smoke. Witnesses saw the meteor explode north of the town of Alliance, followed minutes later by a loud boom. Pieces of the meteorite were found days later. It was eventually determined to be a rare type called an eucrite. Nebraska has a lot of meteorites that are found while farmers are plowing their fields, but there have been only three observed falls.

A large portion of the Owasco meteorite

Total known meteorites from Nevada: 155

OTHER NOTABLE METEORITES:

Moapa Valley: This 699-gram (1.5 lb.) meteorite is a rare CM1 carbonaceous chondrite, one of only 28 found in the world and the only one found in the United States. It was found by a meteorite hunter in Moapa Valley in 2004.

Quinn Canyon: This 1.45-ton (2,900 lb.) iron IIIAB meteorite was found in 1908 and is said to resemble a (huge) turtle. It was discovered by a prospector looking for the mineral borax.

A large piece of Battle Mountain meteorite

State Capital
Site of mentioned meteorite fall
Site of mentioned meteorite find

Sliced and etched Quinn Canyon meteorite

A specimen of Battle Mountain as it was found in the field

BATTLE MOUNTAIN

TYPE: L6 Chondrite
FELL: August 22, 2012
MASS: 2.9+ kilograms (6.38+ lbs.)

Nevada has many meteorite finds because there are dry lake beds throughout the state where meteorites stand out against the flat landscape. Surprisingly, meteorite falls within Nevada are rare, and Battle Mountain is the only meteorite fall that has been found. It fell on August 22, 2012, with only a few witnesses because of its remoteness. A nearby radar station managed to capture data about the fall, giving hunters clues about where the meteorite might have landed. The first piece was found on September 1, and over the next months about two dozen stones were found over hilly and rocky terrain.

New Hampshire

Concord

★ State Capital

Site of mentioned meteorite fall

Site of mentioned meteorite find

Fall leaf cover makes finding meteorites difficult.

METEOR-WRONG: DESERT VARNISH

Another common meteor-wrong would be rocks with desert varnish, a dark polished-looking coating that can be found on rocks in desert regions. It is caused by chemical reactions of particles sticking to and reacting with the surface of a rock in dry environments. Desert varnish won't be found in New Hampshire, but it is important for meteorite hunters to know about.

Rocks with desert varnish

NO METEORITES HAVE BEEN FOUND IN NEW HAMPSHIRE

New Hampshire is in New England, and like other states in the region, its conditions make it difficult to find meteorites. The state has a humid climate throughout the year, which means that meteorites rust and turn to dust fairly quickly. Also, 81 percent of the state is forest, which makes spotting meteorites more difficult. The best areas to look are old rock walls, which are made of rocks moved by farmers out of fields. Since meteorites tend to be heavy, there's a chance that one is being used as a doorstop. It's also possible that a fresh meteorite will land in the state, so be sure to keep an eye on those night skies!

A forest in New Hampshire

Total known meteorites from New Jersey: 1

METEOR-WRONG: SLAG

A very common meteor-wrong is a material called slag. Slag is the byproduct of the industrial melting of rocks. It can have a glassy appearance, or it may look like fusion crust. It is also usually heavy and often contains metals that will attract magnets. Slag is dumped in many places, and often people will randomly come across it and think they have found a meteorite. There is a lot of slag in many states.

Example of slag

The Deal meteorite

SIDE NOTE:

On January 11, 2019, two sisters discovered a crater on Silver Beach, New Jersey. The crater was 5 feet wide and had a dark rock embedded in the center of it. While there was suspicion it might be a meteorite, it turned out to be a piece of coal. It is likely someone made the crater the previous night as a prank.

New Jersey has only one documented meteorite, which fell early in the morning of August 15, 1829. It was seen as a bright meteor, with fiery particles trailing behind. It exploded over Monmouth County, with a local farmer reporting a sound described as louder than muskets and the "whistling of bullets," followed by the noise of objects hitting the ground. Several fragments were found. The largest was taken to New York City and never seen again, but the second piece was sent to the Academy of Natural Sciences in Philadelphia and weighed 28 grams (0.06 lbs.).

The Deal meteorite next to its old label

DEAL

TYPE: L6 Chondrite
FELL: August 15, 1829
MASS: 28 grams (0.06 lbs.)

WILLIAM S. VAUX COLLECTION
ACADEMY OF NATURAL SCIENCES OF PHILADELPHIA, No. 243

STONE - C₁   CHONDRITE
DEAL
...UTH CO., N.J.

State Capital
Site of mentioned meteorite fall
Site of mentioned meteorite find

New Mexico

★ Sante Fe

Glorieta Mountain

Melrose

Portales Valley

★ State Capital

Site of mentioned meteorite fall

Site of mentioned meteorite find

Small crystals of olivines in etched nickel
iron of the Glorieta Mountain meteorite

A slice of Glorieta Mountain meteorite,
with olivine crystals

Total known meteorites from New Mexico: 228

OTHER NOTABLE METEORITES:

Melrose (a): This 36.4-kilogram (80 lb.) L5 chondrite was found in 1933, and it was determined that it contained gold. The meteoriticist Harvey Nininger had samples assayed, which indicated that it contained up to 0.3 ounces of gold per ton. It is not to be confused with Melrose (b), which is a 50-gram (0.1 lb.) howardite found in the same area in 1971.

Portales Valley: A shower of meteorites occurred shortly after a large detonation near Portales on June 13, 1998, and at least 53 specimens of this H6 chondrite were recovered, weighing 71.4 kilograms (157 lbs.).

GLORIETA MOUNTAIN

TYPE: Pallasite PMG-an
FOUND: 1884
MASS: 148+ kilograms (325 lbs.)

In 1884, a prospector found a large metallic rock in three pieces, with a total weight of 143 kilograms (317 lbs.). It was identified as a meteorite. Dozens more pieces were found in the surrounding area over the next century. The meteorite was named Glorieta Mountain, and it turned out to be a pallasite, even though it had a higher metal-to-olivine ratio than most other pallasites. Many of the olivine crystals are gem quality, with attractive apple-green colors. The gem name for olivine is peridot, and sometimes pallasite olivine is cut into gemstones.

A fragment of the Melrose (a) meteorite

Total known meteorites from New York: **11**

OTHER NOTABLE METEORITES:

Schenectady: This 283-gram (0.62 lb.) H5 chondrite fell on April 12, 1968. The homeowner heard a sound on his roof but thought it was a prank. He noticed roof damage and found the meteorite by his house two days later.

Burlington: This 68-kilogram (149 lb.) meteorite was found by a farmer plowing a field in 1819. He took it to a blacksmith to work it into various tools for his use. Only 5 kilograms (11 lbs.) were saved. It is New York's largest meteorite and is an Iron IIIE.

Professor Mark Anders of the Lamont-Doherty Earth Observatory of Columbia University showing the trajectory of the Peekskill meteorite as it hit the car

State Capital

Site of mentioned meteorite fall

Site of mentioned meteorite find

Right: The main mass of the Peekskill meteorite

Below: A slice of the Peekskill meteorite

One of the most famous meteorite falls in the United States occurred on the evening of October 9, 1992. A meteor was recorded on sixteen videos as it flew over the eastern part of the country and was witnessed by thousands of people. The meteorite landed with a bang into a parked car, a 1980 Chevy Malibu, in Peekskill, New York. The meteorite was an H6 chondrite and weighed 12.57 kilograms (27.6 lbs.). It was quickly found by the car's owner, Michelle Knapp. The meteorite was sold to several meteorite dealers, and the car, which originally cost $300, was sold to a meteorite dealer for $25,000. The Chevy has since been displayed in museums around the world.

PEEKSKILL

TYPE: H6 Chondrite
FELL: October 9, 1992
MASS: 12.57 kilograms (27.6 lbs.)

The Schenectady meteorite

North Carolina

The Farmville meteorite, with a sliced section

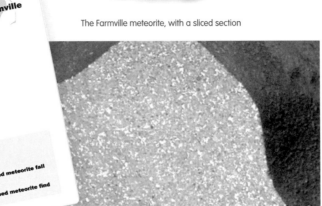

Close-up of Farmville meteorite

Total known meteorites from North Carolina: 29

OTHER NOTABLE METEORITES:

Moore County: This 1,880-gram (4.1 lb.) eucrite meteorite fell on April 21, 1913. It was kept by its finder until being sold to the Smithsonian for $100 during the Great Depression.

Castalia: This 7.3-kilogram (16 lb.) H5 chondrite fell on May 14, 1874. Dozens of small fragments fell over the area.

★ State Capital

Site of mentioned meteorite fall

Site of mentioned meteorite find

FARMVILLE

TYPE: H4 Chondrite
FELL: December 4, 1934
MASS: 56 kilograms (123 lbs.)

A meteor was spotted around 1 p.m. in the afternoon of December 4, 1934, moving east across North Carolina. It exploded over Pitt County, startling the residents. A man near Farmville saw a cloud of dust in a farm field and went to investigate, finding a 5.8-kilogram (12.7 lb.) meteorite embedded 2 feet in the ground. A larger specimen of the same meteorite was found in a cornfield two months later. It weighed 50 kilograms (110 lbs.) and had blasted out a 6-foot-wide crater. The meteorite was an H4 chondrite.

A piece of the Moore County eucrite

Total known meteorites from North Dakota: 11

OTHER NOTABLE METEORITES:

Bowesmont: This 2.27-kilogram (5 lb.) meteorite was found near Bowesmont in 1962 and was an L6 chondrite. In 1972, another 1.3-kilogram (2.8 lb.) meteorite was found in the same area. This may be a separate old fall and has been called Bowesmont (b), an L5 chondrite.

Colgate: In 1999, a large meteorite was found by Tod Erickson during an excavation before construction. It turned out to be an H4 chondrite weighing 39 kilograms (85 lbs.), the largest single meteorite found in North Dakota to date.

A specimen of the Richardton meteorite

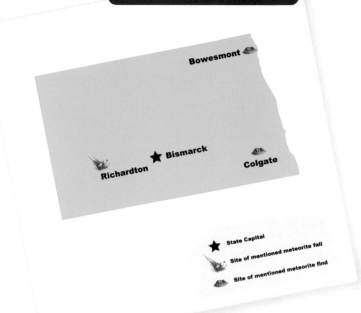

State Capital
Site of mentioned meteorite fall
Site of mentioned meteorite find

On June 30, 1918, a fireball coming from the southeast appeared in the skies of North Dakota. It was reportedly as bright as a roman candle, and it violently exploded near the town of Richardton. Fragments of the meteorite were heard whistling through the air. Some pieces rattled as they landed on the metal roofs of barns. Over a hundred pieces of the meteorite were found over the next few weeks, with the largest weighing 8.3 kilograms (18 lbs.). Collectors quickly arrived in the area and paid as much as $15 per pound ($300 in 2022). It turned out to be an H5 chondrite and is North Dakota's only documented fall.

Thin section of the Bowesmont meteorite

RICHARDTON

TYPE: H5 Chondrite
FELL: June 30, 1918
MASS: 90 kilograms (198 lbs.)

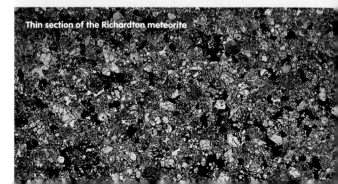

Thin section of the Richardton meteorite

Ohio

A portion of the New Concord meteorite

Total known meteorites from Ohio: 12

OTHER NOTABLE METEORITES:

Fairfield: This 1,600-gram (3.5 lb.) Iron IAB-mg meteorite was found in September 1974 in a gravel pit 120 feet deep. The gravel pit is made of glacial material from the Pleistocene age.

Powellsville: This 4.31-kilogram (9.5 lb.) H5 chondrite was found in 1990 by a man digging out a tree stump in his yard.

State Capital

Site of mentioned meteorite fall

Site of mentioned meteorite find

NEW CONCORD

TYPE: L6 Chondrite
FELL: May 1, 1860
MASS: 230 kilograms (506 lbs.)

An etched piece of the Fairfield meteorite

Ohio's first documented meteorite fall occurred on May 1, 1860. It was well documented because people from Virginia to Ohio were startled by a loud noise, similar to a cannon firing, and witnesses saw stones striking land, buildings, and fences. This was the largest meteorite fall in the United States at that time, and over 30 stones were found. The researcher J. Lawrence Smith mapped the location of two dozen of these stones, creating the first strewn field map for a US meteorite fall. The largest meteorite, which turned out to be an L6 chondrite, weighed 46.8 kilograms (103 lbs.) and was embedded 2 feet deep in the earth.

Total known meteorites from Oklahoma: 40

OTHER NOTABLE METEORITES:

Crescent: This 78.4-gram (0.17 lb.) CM2 carbonaceous chondrite fell during sunset on August 17, 1936. Meteorite hunters used observations to try to locate where the meteorite had fallen, including a report of cows staring in one direction after a loud detonation was heard.

Beaver: This 25.63-kilogram (56 lb.) L5 chondrite was being used as a doorstop at a county jail for over 40 years before it was recognized as a meteorite in 1981.

A specimen of the Crescent meteorite

★ State Capital
Site of mentioned meteorite fall
Site of mentioned meteorite find

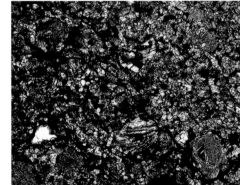

Thin section of the Beaver meteorite

LAKE MURRAY

TYPE: Iron IIAB
FOUND: 1933
MASS: 270 kilograms (594 lbs.)

A slice of the Lake Murray meteorite

In 1933 a farmer named J. C. Dodson found a large iron mass on his farm in a gully. The farm was sold to the state of Oklahoma and became part of Lake Murray State Park. In 1952 Mr. Dodson was visiting the park and talked to geologist Allen Graffham about the meteorite. They took a short walk to the gully, and it was still there. The next day they and other researchers excavated the meteorite, which was embedded in a Cretaceous sandstone, indicating the meteorite had landed back then and was buried. There was a 6-inch layer of weathered rusty iron around the meteorite, but the core was still iron-nickel and weighed 560 lbs. The meteorite likely weighed 3,040 lbs. when it first landed 110 million years ago.

Oregon

The Willamette meteorite shortly after it was excavated

State Capital

Site of mentioned meteorite fall

Site of mentioned meteorite find

A specimen of the Salem meteorite

Total known meteorites from Oregon: 6

OTHER NOTABLE METEORITES:

Salem: Oregon's only fall produced a 61.4-gram (0.13 lb.) L6 chondrite that fell on the roof of a house in 1981. It landed only a few feet away from a police officer.

Fitzwater Pass: This 65.4-gram (0.14 lb.) Iron IIIF meteorite was found in a grassy area near a mountaintop in 1974. It is one of only nine Iron IIIF meteorites. Surprisingly, another Iron IIIF meteorite called Klamath Falls was found only 78 kilometers (48 miles) away in 1952, but it is not believed to be from the same fall.

WILLAMETTE

TYPE: Iron IIIAB
FOUND: 1902 (though known earlier to local tribes)
MASS: 15.5 tons (31,000 lbs.)

The largest known in the United States, this 15.5-ton (31,000 lb.) meteorite is believed to have fallen on an ice sheet covering Montana or Canada during the Ice Age; it was rafted down into the Willamette River valley approximately 13,000 years ago, during the Missoula Floods. It was known as Tomanowos to the Indigenous Clackamas people, who revered it and collected the rainwater trapped on the meteorite for their traditions and ceremonies. In 1902, a settler found it on a neighbor's land and secretly moved it to his own as a tourist attraction. The original landowner found out and sued to gain custody of it. Eventually it was purchased and donated to the American Museum of Natural History. The museum has an agreement with the descendants of the Clackamas to allow access to the meteorite for ceremonies and to return the meteorite if it goes off display.

The Willamette meteorite on display at the American Museum of Natural History in New York City

Total known meteorites from Pennsylvania: 8

OTHER NOTABLE METEORITES:

Pittsburgh: In 1850, a farmer picked up a rock to throw at a snake and found it to be surprisingly heavy. Part of the rock weighing 600 grams (1.32 lbs.) was sent to be studied, and it was found to be an Iron IAB-mg meteorite. The rest was taken to a blacksmith and forged into an iron bar.

Mount Joy: This 384-kilogram (845 lb.) Iron IIAB meteorite was found in 1887 and is the largest meteorite in Pennsylvania to date. It was found by someone digging a hole to plant an apple tree.

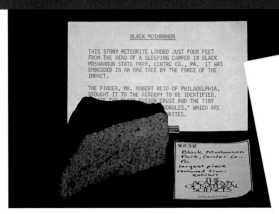

BLACK MOSHANNON

THIS STONY METEORITE LANDED JUST FOUR FEET FROM THE HEAD OF A SLEEPING CAMPER IN BLACK MOSHANNON STATE PARK, CENTRE CO., PA. IT WAS EMBEDDED IN AN OAK TREE BY THE FORCE OF THE IMPACT.

THE FINDER, MR. ROBERT REID OF PHILADELPHIA, BROUGHT IT TO THE ACADEMY TO BE IDENTIFIED. ... THE BLACK FUSION CRUST AND THE TINY ... DRULES," WHICH ARE ... RITES.

The main mass of Black Moshannan Park

Ward's Natural Science Establishment,
Mount Joy Found 1887
Adams County, Pennsylvania
76-104 College Ave., Rochester, N.Y.

A fragment of Mount Joy

A cross section of Mount Joy

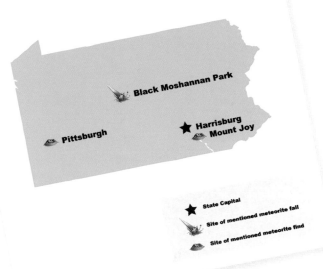

Black Moshannan Park

Pittsburgh

Harrisburg
Mount Joy

★ State Capital

Site of mentioned meteorite fall

Site of mentioned meteorite find

BLACK MOSHANNAN PARK

TYPE: L5 Chondrite
FELL: July 10, 1941
MASS: 705 grams (1.5 lbs.)

Robert H. Reed and his family were camping in Black Moshannan State Park in Pennsylvania in early July when, on the morning of July 10, 1941, he heard what was described as "a million bumblebees." The noise grew louder until he heard a dull thud and saw leaves and twigs fall from nearby trees. He went to the site and dug out a small hand-sized stone that turned out to be an L5 chondritic meteorite. Several other stones were recovered later.

Rhode Island

Providence ★

★ State Capital

Site of mentioned meteorite fall

Site of mentioned meteorite find

Meteor-wrong: Basalt

Basalt is a volcanic rock that is dark and usually has holes or vesicles. It is often mistaken for a meteorite based on its appearance. Sometimes basalt contains pieces of other rocks, including rocks made of olivine, making it look almost like pallasites. There is not much basalt in Rhode Island but it's a rock to be aware of.

House on a beach in Rhode Island

An example of basalt with olivine crystals

NO METEORITES HAVE BEEN FOUND IN RHODE ISLAND

Rhode Island is the smallest state in the United States by land area, with 1,214 square miles of forests, beaches, and towns. The state contains a lot of coastline, which means there's a good chance that meteorites have landed in the water and have never been found. As a New England state, Rhode Island also has a wetter climate that makes it difficult for meteorites to survive long, because they quickly erode. Meteorites also don't last long on beaches. The best areas to look for meteorites in this state would be in old rock walls and near farmland. Because meteorites are heavy, they are often used as doorstops, so one may be sitting around in a house somewhere. Of course, a fresh meteorite could land in the state, so never count out the possibility when you see a bright flash in the sky.

Total known meteorites from South Carolina: 7

OTHER NOTABLE METEORITES:

Cherokee Springs: This 8.4-kilogram (18.5 lb.) LL6 chondrite fell on July 1, 1933. One piece struck the limb of a tree before hitting the ground, and another piece landed near a barn.

Ruff's Mountain: This 53.07-kilogram (116 lb.) Iron IIIAB meteorite was found in 1844. It is the largest ever found in South Carolina to date.

Slice of a fragment of Cherokee Springs

State Capital

Site of mentioned meteorite fall

Site of mentioned meteorite find

A fragment of the Bishopville aubrite

BISHOPVILLE

TYPE: Aubrite
FELL: March 25, 1843
MASS: 6 kilograms (13.2 lbs.)

South Carolina's first meteorite fall and find occurred on March 25, 1843, when a meteor was witnessed over the skies of eastern South Carolina. It exploded near Bishopville, and a large 6-kilogram (13.2 lb.) stone was recovered. The stone was unusual, having a glassy crust and white interior. Initially, it was described as a new class of meteorite called "chladnite," but it was later classified as an aubrite (the first aubrite had fallen years earlier in Aubres, France). Aubrites contain large crystalline masses of the mineral enstatite. They are rare, and only five have been found in the United States.

South Dakota

Lemmon

Bath

★ Pierre

Centerville

State Capital
Site of mentioned meteorite fall
Site of mentioned meteorite find

Thin section of the
Centerville meteorite

Total known meteorites from South Dakota: 19

OTHER NOTABLE METEORITES:

Centerville: South Dakota's second meteorite fall occurred on February 29, 1956, and a stone fell through the roof of a shed on the McMurchie Ranch and struck a corn planter. It was a 45-gram (0.1 lb.) H5 chondrite.

Lemmon: In 1984, a woman found a 6.6-kilogram (14.5 lb.) stone next to a fence post and placed it along her driveway border. In 1998, it was recognized by someone who was going door to door looking for meteorites. It was then determined to be an H5 chondrite.

BATH

TYPE: H4 Chondrite
FELL: August 29, 1892
MASS: 21 kilograms (46 lbs.)

A specimen of the Bath meteorite

South Dakota's first meteorite fall occurred on August 29, 1892. On that afternoon, a farmer named Lawrence Freeman and his son heard a series of explosions and saw a meteor falling through the sky, trailed by smoke. It landed 330 feet from where they were standing and buried itself 16 inches in the ground. It turned out to be a 21-kilogram (46 lb.) H4 chondrite.

A piece of the Lemmon meteorite

Total known meteorites from Tennessee: 25

OTHER NOTABLE METEORITES:

Charlotte: The first iron-meteorite fall in the United States occurred on July 31, 1835. It landed in a cotton field but wasn't found until the field was plowed in the fall. It was a 4.3-kilogram (9.4 lb.) Iron IVA meteorite.

Maryville: This 1,443-gram (3.1 lb.) L6 meteorite fell on the morning of January 28, 1983, and was found by Mary Green, a schoolteacher, in her backyard.

A slice of the Charlotte meteorite

State Capital
Site of mentioned meteorite fall
Site of mentioned meteorite find

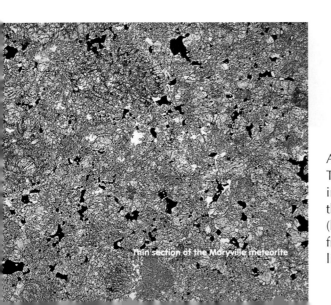

Thin section of the Maryville meteorite

The Petersburg eucrite

PETERSBURG

TYPE: Eucrite
FELL: August 5, 1855
MASS: 1.8 kilograms (3.9 lbs.)

At 3:30 p.m. on August 5, 1855, a meteor arrived with a noise like cannon fire in southeastern Tennessee. It was described as having a 2-foot-wide luminous halo, and it embedded itself 18 inches into the ground. It had a thin, black, shining crust with numerous flow lines. It turned out that the 1.8-kilogram (3.9 lb.) meteorite is an eucrite member of the HED group of meteorites (howardite-eucrite-diogenite). In the 20th century, scientists postulated that HED meteorites were from the asteroid 4 Vesta, having been knocked off 4 Vesta by a larger impact hundreds of millions of years ago.

Texas

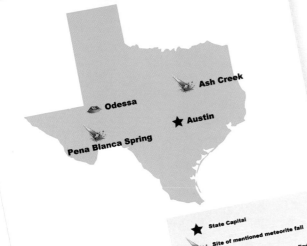

State Capital

Site of mentioned meteorite fall

Site of mentioned meteorite find

A specimen of the Ash Creek meteorite

Total known meteorites from Texas: 313

OTHER NOTABLE METEORITES:

Ash Creek: On February 15, 2009, a meteor was observed by many people in the swath of land from Austin to Ft. Worth, Texas. Weather Doppler radar recorded the track of the meteor, prompting meteorite hunters to descend on the likeliest strewn field. One of the first meteorites found may have been by Hopper, a stray border collie who picked up a 70-gram (0.15 lb.) specimen in the area. Over 9.5 kilos (20.9 lbs.) of this L6 chondrite was eventually found.

Peña Blanca Spring: A loud explosion preceded a meteor that fell into a pool of water on August 2, 1946. It made a huge splash that wet things up to 100 feet away. It was a 70-kilogram (154 lb.) aubrite meteorite and was recovered in pieces from the water.

ODESSA

TYPE: Iron IAB-mg
FOUND: 1922
MASS: 1.6 tons+ (3,200+ lbs.)

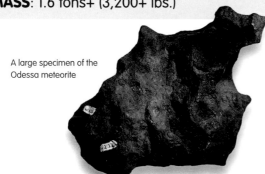

A large specimen of the Odessa meteorite

Southwest of the city of Odessa is a shallow meteor crater measuring 550 feet wide but only 15 feet deep. It was likely 100 feet deep when the impact occurred 62,000 years ago, but over the millennia the crater has filled with soil. The site was identified as a meteor crater in the 1920s, and hundreds of small iron meteorites have been dug out of the surrounding terrain in the decades since. The meteor crater is designated a national natural landmark by the US Park Service, and there is a visitor center on-site. There are four other smaller buried craters in the area from the same impact.

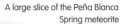

A large slice of the Peña Blanca Spring meteorite

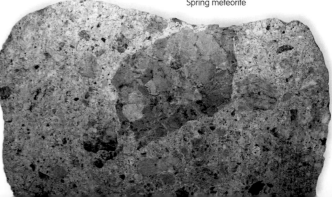

Total known meteorites from Utah: 26

OTHER NOTABLE METEORITES:

Garland: Utah's only recovered meteorite fall came in the summer of 1950. A woman was gardening when she heard a hissing sound and thud. She then discovered a small black stone only 3 feet away from her. It turned out to be a 102-gram (0.2 lb.) diogenite, a member of the HED group of meteorites.

Ioka: This 31.5-kilogram (69 lb.) L3.5 chondrite was found in 1931.

The Drum Mountain meteorite

Garland

★ Salt Lake City

Ioka

Drum Mountains

★ State Capital

Site of mentioned meteorite fall

Site of mentioned meteorite find

The Ioka meteorite

DRUM MOUNTAIN

TYPE: Iron IIIAB
FOUND: 1944
MASS: 529 kilograms (1,164 lbs.)

The Topaz War Relocation Center at Drum Mountain was an internment camp for Japanese Americans and immigrants from 1942 to 1945. Two internees, Akio Ujihara and Yoshio Nishimoto, were looking for chalcedony in the area for lapidary work when they came upon a large iron mass measuring 2.5 feet long. Suspecting that it might be a meteorite, they sent a piece to the National Museum (what is now the Smithsonian Museum of Natural History), which confirmed that it was a meteorite—and the largest meteorite from Utah. The 529-kilogram (1,164 lb.) Iron IIIAB meteorite was soon brought to the museum for display and research, and the finders were paid $700. It took 56 hours to saw off a section of a meteorite for study.

Vermont

Montpelier ★

★ State Capital

Site of mentioned meteorite fall

Site of mentioned meteorite find

NO METEORITES HAVE BEEN FOUND IN VERMONT

View from Jonesville, Vermont, with Mount Mansfield in the distance

Meteor-wrong: Magnetite

Magnetite is a mineral that is commonly mistaken as a meteorite. It contains a lot of iron, and therefore it is attracted to a magnet and will set off metal detectors. It is also dark in color and heavy. It can be found in many states throughout the US. There are other metallic minerals such as hematite that are also meteor-wrongs.

An example of magnetite

SIDE NOTE

In August 1942, a 5-pound iron mass was found in South Strafford and was believed to be a meteorite. There is no additional information about this find, although it is probably a pseudometeorite—an object that looks like a meteorite but isn't.

Vermont is a New England state and, like its neighbor New Hampshire, falls within a region with conditions that make it difficult to find meteorites. The state's humid climate means that meteorites erode to dust fairly quickly. The state is 78 percent forest, which makes it difficult for meteorite hunters to spot what they are looking for. The annual snowfall is 60 to 100 inches, and Vermont is the seventh-coldest state in the country. The best areas to look for meteorites are in old rock walls, where farmers have moved rocks to clear fields. There's always the chance that a fresh meteorite might fall within the state's boundaries. Meteorites are often used as doorstops and garden decorations, so one might just be sitting around in an old homestead near you.

Total known meteorites from Virginia: 13

Virginia

OTHER NOTABLE METEORITES:

Lorton: On January 18, 2010, a meteorite smashed through a roof and into a doctor's office. The 330-gram (0.72 lb.) L6 chondrite filled an examination room and hallway with debris.

Sharps: This 1,265-gram (3 lb.) H3.4 chondrite fell on April 1, 1921. It landed just 100 yards away from the person who found it.

A fragment of the Richmond meteorite

★ State Capital
Site of mentioned meteorite fall
Site of mentioned meteorite find

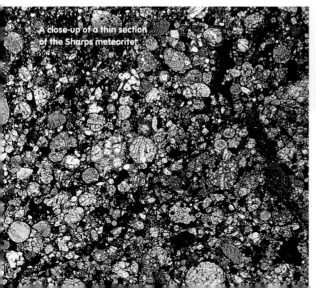

A close-up of a thin section of the Sharps meteoritet

Portion of the Lorton meteorite and the ceiling tile it smashed through

RICHMOND

TYPE: LL5 Chondrite
FELL: June 4, 1828
MASS: 1,800 grams (3.9 lbs.)

On June 4, 1828, Virginia's first meteorite fall and find was heard as an explosion southwest of Richmond. It was reported to sound like a cannon, before the noise of a heavy object hit the earth. Searchers went to the location and found a hole in the earth with a stone buried 12 inches deep. The meteorite turned out to be an LL5 chondrite.

Washington

State Capital
Site of mentioned meteorite fall
Site of mentioned meteorite find

The Withrow meteorite

Total known meteorites from Washington: 6

OTHER NOTABLE METEORITES:

Withrow: A 8.73-kilogram (19.2 lb.) Iron IIIAB? (yes, the classification has a question mark because it has not been carefully analyzed) meteorite was found lying on the surface of the earth. It was located only 5 miles from the Waterville meteorite, but research has determined that they are not related.

Washougal: This 225-gram (0.5 lb.) howardite meteorite fell on July 2, 1939. It is Washington state's only documented recovered fall.

WATERVILLE

TYPE: Iron IAB-ung
FOUND: 1917
MASS: 37.13 kilograms (81 lbs.)

The Waterville meteorite

In 1917, a large iron mass was found on the Fachnie farm, near the town of Waterville. Mr. Fachnie was harvesting wheat when the wheat binder hit the meteorite. Scientists initially thought that it had fallen the year before, but the level of corrosion on the meteorite indicated that it had been in the ground for a much longer time. It turned out to be an Iron IAB-ung, the first and largest meteorite found in the state of Washington.

63

Total known meteorites from West Virginia: 3

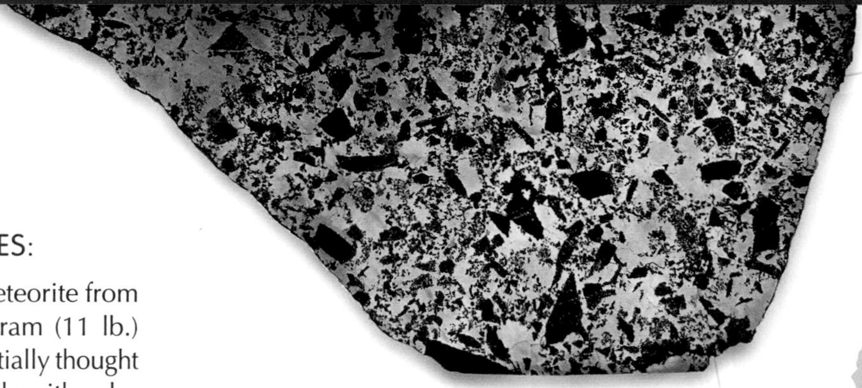

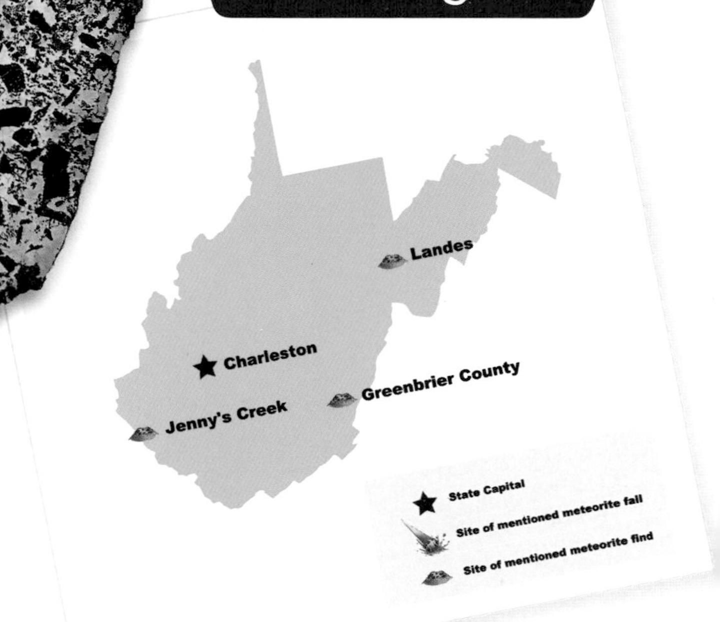

OTHER NOTABLE METEORITES:

Greenbrier County: The first meteorite from in West Virginia was a 5-kilogram (11 lb.) Iron IIAB found in 1880. It was initially thought to be iron ore and taken to a blacksmith, who heated it and chiseled it into several pieces.

Jenny's Creek: Three highly oxidized fragments totaling 12 kilograms (26.4 lbs.) were found in the same area in 1883 and 1885. They turned out to be from an Iron IAB-mg meteorite.

A slice of the Landes meteorite

Landes

Charleston

Jenny's Creek

Greenbrier County

State Capital

Site of mentioned meteorite fall

Site of mentioned meteorite find

Fragments of the Jenny's Creek meteorite

LANDES

TYPE: Iron IAB-mg
FOUND: 1930
MASS: 69.8 kilograms (153 lbs.)

In 1930, V. A. Stump was plowing a field on his farm when he plowed up a large iron mass. He put it under the eaves of his barn, where it sat until 1968, when it was brought to the attention of the meteoriticist Gless Huss. Surprisingly, water was dripping on the meteorite during this time, but there was no damage. The iron meteorite, which is an Iron IAM-mg, turned out to be the largest found in West Virginia to date. It has an interesting interior, with silicate inclusions in coarse octahedrite nickel-iron.

Wisconsin

Total known meteorites from Wisconsin: 14

OTHER NOTABLE METEORITES:

Trenton: Around 1858, a farmer plowed up four large masses of iron; within the next few years, several others were plowed up. These turned out to be an Iron IIIAB meteorite, which together weighed 505 kilograms (1,112 lbs.).

Belmont: This H6 chondrite was plowed up in 1958 and weighed 25.3 kilograms (55 lbs.). A portion of the meteorite was sent for study to Dr. Lincoln LaPaz at the University of New Mexico. Aside from his work with meteorites, Dr. LaPaz is known for UFO research for the US government, specifically green fireballs.

Trenton

Belmont

Madison

Mifflin

★ State Capital

Site of mentioned meteorite fall

Site of mentioned meteorite find

A slice of the
Belmont meteorite

MIFFLIN

TYPE: L5 Chondrite
FELL: April 14, 2010
MASS: 3.58 kilograms (7.8 lbs.)

On the evening of April 14, 2010, a bright meteor was seen over Wisconsin, Iowa, and Illinois. It was also caught on camera and Doppler radar. A large explosion was heard over the town of Mifflin, and soon after, meteorite hunters descended on the area. On April 15, a 7.4-gram (0.016 lb.) stone was found on the roof of a shed. Over the next few weeks, more than 70 meteorites were recovered throughout a strewn field 13 miles long. The meteorite turned out to be an L5 chondrite, with the largest stone weighing 332 grams (0.73 lbs.).

A specimen of the Mifflin meteorite in the field

Wyoming

Total known meteorites from Wyoming: 14

OTHER NOTABLE METEORITES:

Torrington: An H6 chondrite fell in Wyoming on September 23, 1944, during World War II. It is the state's only documented meteorite fall. By the time a researcher arrived to investigate, only three stones weighing 259 grams (0.57 lbs.) were recovered, although originally there had been more.

Bear Lodge: This 48.5-kilogram (106 lb.) Iron IIIAB meteorite was found in 1931 by a worker repairing a highway near Bear Lodge Mountain.

A slice of the Torrington meteorite

Bear Lodge

Torrington
Albin
Cheyenne

★ State Capital
Site of mentioned meteorite fall
Site of mentioned meteorite find

A slice of the Albin pallasite

ALBIN

TYPE: Pallasite PMG
FOUND: 1915
MASS: 37.6 kilograms (82 lbs.)

There are only 50 meteorites of the Pallasite PMG type in the world, and the Albin meteorite is one of only nine found in the United States. It was found by a rancher in 1915 but wasn't recognized as a meteorite until 1935. The meteorite had a flat disc and contained yellow-orange crystals of olivine in nickel iron.

A section of the Albin pallasite

APPENDIX: METEORITE CLASSIFICATION

Here are descriptions of the categories referenced under "Type" for each meteorite.

STONY METEORITES

Stony meteorites are divided into the chondrites and the achondrites.

CHONDRITES

There are several classes and groups of chondrites, and each group likely originated from a separate asteroid.

Ordinary chondrites: The most common chondrite; has three groups:

H: has high levels of iron

L: has low levels of iron

LL: has very low metal content; can barely be picked up by a magnet

Enstatite: A chondrite containing a lot of the mineral enstatite; has two groups:

EH: has high levels of iron

EL: has low levels of iron

Carbonaceous: A class of chondrites that contain more carbon than other chondrites, up to 5 percent. Carbonaceous chondrites are important to science because they contain organic compounds, calcium-aluminum-rich inclusions from early in the solar system, and exotic minerals. They are divided into several groups, based on their composition:

CI: Ivuna group: named for the Ivuna meteorite that fell in Tanzania in 1938

CM: Mighei group: named for the Mighei meteorite that fell in Ukraine in 1889

CV: Vigarano group: named for the Vigarano meteorite that fell in Italy in 1910

CR: Renazzo group: named for the Renazzo meteorite that fell in Italy in 1824

CO: Ornans group: named for the Ornans meteorite that fell in France in 1868

CK: Karoonda group: named for the Karoonda meteorite that fell in Australia in 1930

CB: Bencubbin group: named for the Bencubbin meteorite that fell in Australia in 1930

CH: A high-iron group: a group that has over 20 percent nickel-iron

C-ung: Ungrouped carbonaceous that don't belong with the others

Rumuruti group: This group uses the symbol R; its members are named after the Rumuruti meteorite that fell in Kenya in 1934. They have almost no iron metal.

Kakangari group: This group uses the symbol K and are named for the Kakangari meteorite that fell in India in 1890. They are chemically different from the other chondrites.

ACHONDRITES

Achondrites are rocky meteorites that are divided into several classes and groups, which indicate different original-source asteroids.

The **HED meteorite class:** HED stands for howardite-eucrite-diogenite, the three members of this group. Study of the HED group suggests that they came from the huge asteroid 4 Vesta, a 326-mile-wide asteroid in the asteroid belt. Most achondrites are from the HED group.

howardites: A group named after the British chemist and meteorite researcher Edward C. Howard. It's a regolith breccia: a rock formed from broken mixed-up rock resulting from meteor impacts on a planet or an asteroid's surface

eucrites: A group that is composed of basaltic rock from the crust of 4 Vesta. Its name comes from the Greek word *eukritos*, meaning "easily distinguished."

diogenites: A group composed of igneous rock that likely comes from deeper in the crust of 4 Vesta. Often, this group has dark-green crystals of various minerals. Named after the ancient Greek philosopher Diogenes.

Angrite group: Named after the Angra dos Reis meteorite that fell in Brazil in 1869. It is composed of basaltic rock with small holes or vesicles and contains a lot of the mineral augite and some other minerals.

Aubrite group: Named after the Aubres meteorite that fell in France in 1836. It is composed mostly of the mineral orthopyroxene enstatite and has a light-colored interior.

Ureilite group: Named after the Novo-Urei meteorite that fell in Russia in 1886. This group contains a lot of carbon, sometimes in the form of microscopic diamonds.

Brachinite group: Named after the Brachina meteorite that was found in Australia in 1974. This is an odd group that is almost entirely composed of fine grains of olivine.

PRIMITIVE ACHONDRITES

This group of achondrites is composed of melted chondrites that still retain some of the characteristics of chondrites. They have chemical elements similar to chondrites. Members of this group include the following:

Acapulcoites. Named after the Acapulco meteorite that fell in Mexico in 1976, its chemical composition is similar to chondrites and occasionally has some chondrules.

Lodranites: Named after the Lodran meteorite that fell in Pakistan in 1868, it has the same composition as Acapulcoites but larger grains.

Winonaites: Named after the Winona meteorite that was found in Arizona in 1928, its chemistry is similar to chondrites, but it also has veins of melted metal.

Lunar meteorites: Large meteor impacts on the Moon will knock off chunks of rock that may make their way to Earth as meteorites. The first one was found in Antarctica in 1979; since then, over 300 lunar meteorites have been discovered. All lunar achondrites are considered to be the same group. There are, however, different kinds of lunar meteorite, including types of breccias, basalts, and anorthosites.

Martian meteorites: As with the Moon, large meteor impacts occasionally knock pieces of Mars into space; some make their way to Earth as meteorites. Martian meteorites are divided into three main types, known as the SNC (shergottites, nakhlites, and chassignites):

Shergottites: Named for the Shergotty meteorite that fell in India in 1865, this type is an igneous rock.

Nakhlites: Named for the Nakhla meteorite that fell in Egypt in 1911, these are rich in the mineral augite and may have been formed in volcanic events.

Chassignites: Named from the Chassigny meteorite that fell in France in 1815, these are composed of 90 percent iron-rich olivine.

Ungrouped Martian meteorites: There are many meteorites with chemistry that shows that they're from Mars, but they do not fit in to the three main types listed above. The most famous example is Allan Hills 84001, found in Antarctica in 1984. In 1996, scientists announced that they found evidence of fossil bacteria in the meteorite; most scientists disagree with this finding.

Ungrouped: There are many achondrites that do not fall into any of the above categories; they should therefore be considered ungrouped.

IRON METEORITES

Iron meteorites are an alloy of iron-nickel, with the majority being iron, and the nickel ranging from 6 to 16+ percent nickel. Iron meteorites used to be classified by their Widmanstätten pattern: hexahedrites, different octahedrites, and ataxites. However, now iron meteorites are grouped by their chemistry, which indicates they're from distinct asteroids.

The current groupings include:

IAB: This group is an iron meteorite but is also considered a primitive achondrite because it shares similar chemistry to Winonaites. Contains subgroups IA and IB.

IC: a small group

IIAB: Another group with many well-recognized iron meteorites. May be related to carbonaceous asteroids. Contains subgroups IIA and IIB

IIC: a small group

IID: a small group

IIE: A small group with a lot of silicate inclusions. May be related to H chondrites.

IIF: a small group

IIG: a small group

IIIAB: This is the largest group of iron meteorites, with over 200 members; it includes some of the largest iron meteorites, such as the Willamette. Contains subgroups IIIA and IIIB.

IIICD: This group has a lot of silicate inclusions and is also considered a primitive achondrite. Likely originated from the same asteroid as Winonaites.

IIIE: a small group

IIIF: a small group

IVA: a medium-sized group

IVB: a small group, although it includes the largest meteorite on Earth: the Hoba meteorite of Namibia, which weighs 60 tons.

Ungrouped Irons: About 15 percent of all iron meteorites do not fit in the above groups.

STONY-IRON METEORITES

Stony-iron meteorites are divided into two groups: pallasites and mesosiderites.

PALLASITES

Pallasites are a group of meteorites that have crystals of olivine in an iron-nickel matrix. They are named after the German naturalist Peter Pallas, who studied a specimen in 1772. Pallasites are believed to be from the core-mantle boundary of large differentiated asteroids that were later shattered by impacts.

There are several subgroups:

Main-Group Pallasites: Or PMG; nearly all pallasites belong to this group. It usually has a mixture of two-thirds olivine crystals and one-third iron-nickel. Olivine crystals measure up to 2 centimeters across. The chemistry of the iron-nickel is similar to that of the IIIAB group of iron meteorites, which suggests they're from the same original asteroid.

Eagle Station Pallasites: Or PES; there are only five meteorites that belong to this group. Their chemistry is similar to IIF iron meteorites.

Ungrouped: There are several pallasites that do not fit the above groups. Several contain the mineral clinopyroxene, and some scientists occasionally refer to them as the pyroxene pallasites, or PPX.

MESOSIDERITES

Mesosiderites are a group of meteorites with a fairly equal mix of silicate minerals and iron-nickel. They are composed of breccias, with mixes of silicates and metals ranging from lumps to fine mixes. The metal has a composition similar to IIIAB iron meteorites, while the silicates are similar to the HED achondrite group.

The group is divided into three classes:

A: This class is basaltic and ranges in "metamorphic grade" from 1 to 4. Grade 1 is fine-grained fragments. Grade 2 and 3 are recrystallized. Grade 4 is a melted-matrix breccia.

B: This class is ultramafic and ranges in metamorphic grade from 1 to 4.

C: This class is orthopyroxene and ranges in metamorphic grade from 1 to 3.

GLOSSARY

ablation: The process in which pieces of a meteor are melted off or knocked off while going through the atmosphere

achondrite: A meteorite type without any chondrules

amino acid: Certain organic compounds

asteroid: A large natural object in space greater than 1 meter (3 feet) but smaller than planets

atoms: The building blocks of all matter, identified as elements

basaltic: Made of basalt, a dark magnesium and iron-rich volcanic rock

carbon: A chemical element that is an important component of life

carbonaceous: A meteorite type that contains more carbon than other meteorites

chemical formula: A representation of the atoms in a molecule

chondrite: A meteorite type with chondrules

chondrules: Tiny, spherical particles of rock

comet: A large natural object in space made of ice and rock; usually comes from farther out than the planet Neptune

core: The metallic center inside a planet or large asteroid

crust: The outer surface of a planet or large asteroid

crater: A depression in the ground excavated by a meteor impact

crystal: The result of a formation of atoms that follow a particular pattern

differentiation/differentiated: The process when an asteroid gets really big and the interior gets hot and melted, resulting in different layers of material (large asteroids and planets are differentiated)

diogenite: A member of the HED group of achondrites, likely from the asteroid 4 Vesta

Doppler radar: A type of radar usually used for weather but can sometimes accidentally capture the passing of large meteors

eucrite: A member of the HED group of achondrites, likely from the asteroid 4 Vesta

fireball: A meteor that is bigger and brighter and lasts longer than most meteors

flow lines: Lines of melted rock on the fusion crust of a meteorite

fusion crust: Thin coating of melted rock on a meteorite, formed as the meteor was heated and ablated in the atmosphere

gravity: A force that causes things to be attracted to each other

hammer: Term for a meteorite that strikes a human-made object

HED: The howardite-eucrite-diogenite group of achondrite meteorites, likely from the asteroid 4 Vesta

howardite: A member of the HED group of achondrites, likely from the asteroid 4 Vesta

igneous: Rocks that are formed out of molten rocks from deep in an asteroid or planet

iron-nickel: Alloy of the elements iron and nickel, common to most meteorites

kamacite: One of the alloys of iron-nickel that can be found in meteorites

main mass: The largest piece of a meteorite

mantle: Area between the core and the crust of an asteroid or planet, usually very hot

mesosiderite: Type of meteorite that is partially metal and partially rock

metamorphic: Type of rock that has undergone transformation due to heat and pressure

meteor: An object falling in the atmosphere, usually bright and called a shooting star

meteoriticist: Scientist who studies meteorites

meteoroid: Natural object in space under 1 meter (3 feet) in size

meteor-wrong: An unofficial term for an object that looks like a meteorite but is not

molecule: A group of atoms that are bonded together

olivine: A group of minerals, often with a green appearance, occasionally used as a gemstone

orbit: The circular or oval path an object in space travels due to gravity

orientation: The position of a meteor as it goes through the atmosphere

pallasite: Type of meteorite that is partially metal and partially olivine

planetesimal: Early objects in the solar system formed by dust and particles gathering together

pseudometeorite: Object that looks like a meteorite but is not

regmaglypts: Dents and dimples on a meteorite's surface

silicon: An element common in many stony meteorites

silicate: A mineral with the element silicon

solar system: A region that includes our sun and the planets

strewn field: The area where meteorites from an exploding meteor fell, usually has an oval shape

taenite: One of the alloys of iron-nickel that can be found in meteorites

trajectory: The direction something is moving

Widmanstätten pattern: A pattern in Iron and Stony-Iron meteorites formed by crystals of iron-nickel (revealed only by careful etching with certain acids)

PLACES TO SEE METEORITES

Meteorites can be found in almost every state, but the best places to see them are in museums. While there are many museums in every state, the ones listed here have meteorites on display or are generally related to geology. There are many more museums not listed, so ask around. Be sure to check visiting hours and information before you go.

ALABAMA
Anniston Museum of Natural History (Anniston)
Alabama Museum of Natural History (Tuscaloosa)

ALASKA
Alaska Museum of Science & Nature (Anchorage)

ARIZONA
Museum of Natural History (Mesa)
Center for Meteorite Studies (ASU Tempe)
University of Arizona Mineral Museum (Tucson)
Meteorite Crater (near Winslow)

ARKANSAS
Arkansas State University Museum (Jonesboro)

CALIFORNIA
Humboldt State University Natural History Museum (Arcata)
Desert Discovery Center (Barstow)
Gateway Science Museum (California State University, Chico)
Fallbrook Gem & Mineral Museum (Fallbrook)
Western Science Center (Hemet)
Natural History Museum, Los Angeles County (Los Angeles)
California State Mining and Mineral Museum (Mariposa)
Sierra College Natural History Museum (Rocklin)
San Diego Natural History Museum (San Diego)
San Diego Mineral, Gem & Fossil Museum (San Diego)
California Academy of Science (San Francisco)
Santa Barbara Museum of Natural History (Santa Barbara)

COLORADO
Western Museum of Mining & Industry (Colorado Springs)
Denver Museum of Nature & Science (Denver)
Colorado School of Mines Geology Museum (Golden)

CONNECTICUT
Bruce Museum (Greenwich)
Connecticut Museum of Mining and Mineral Science (Kent)
Yale Peabody Museum of Natural History (New Haven)

DELAWARE
University of Delaware Mineralogical Museum (Newark)

DISTRICT OF COLUMBIA
Smithsonian National Museum of Natural History

FLORIDA
Gillespie Museum (Deland)
Florida Museum of Natural History (Gainesville)

GEORGIA
Fernbank Museum of Natural History (Atlanta)
Tellus Science Museum (Cartersville)

HAWAII
Bernice Pauahi Bishop Museum (Honolulu)

IDAHO
Idaho Museum of Mining & Geology (Boise)
Idaho Museum of Natural History (Pocatello)

ILLINOIS
Field Museum of Natural History (Chicago)
Burpee Museum of Natural History (Rockford)
Illinois State Museum (Springfield)

INDIANA
Children's Museum of Indianapolis (Indianapolis)
Indiana State Museum (Indianapolis)

IOWA
University of Iowa Museum of Natural History (Iowa City)

KANSAS
Johnston Geology Museum (Emporia)
KU Biodiversity Institute and Natural History Museum (Lawrence)
Museum of World Treasures (Wichita)

KENTUCKY
Kentucky Science Center (Louisville)

LOUISIANA
Museum of Natural Science (Louisiana State University, Baton Rouge)
Lafayette Science Museum (Lafayette)

MAINE
Maine State Museum (Augusta)
Maine Mineral and Gem Museum (Bethel)

MARYLAND
Maryland Science Center (Baltimore)

MASSACHUSETTS
Beneski Museum of Natural History (Amherst)
Harvard Museum of Natural History (Cambridge)
The Mineralogical & Geological Museum at Harvard University (Cambridge)
Berkshire Museum (Pittsfield)

MICHIGAN
University of Michigan Museum of Natural History (Ann Arbor)
Cranbrook Institute of Science (Bloomfield Hills)
Wayne State University Geology Mineral Museum (Detroit)
Michigan State University Museum (East Lansing)
A. E. Seaman Mineral Museum of Michigan Tech (Houghton)
Central Michigan University Museum of Cultural and Natural History (Mount Pleasant)

MINNESOTA
Science Museum of Minnesota (Saint Paul)

MISSISSIPPI
Dunn-Seiler Museum (Starkville)

MISSOURI
Joplin History & Mineral Museum (Joplin)
St. Louis Science Center (St. Louis)

MONTANA
Montana Bureau of Mines & Geology Mineral Museum (Butte)

NEBRASKA
Hastings Museum (Hastings)
University of Nebraska State Museum (Lincoln)

NEVADA
Nevada State Museum (Carson City)
Nevada State Museum (Las Vegas)
Las Vegas Natural History Museum (Las Vegas)
W. M. Keck Earth Science and Mineral Engineering Museum (Reno)

NEW JERSEY
Franklin Mineral Museum (Franklin)
Rutgers University Geology Museum (New Brunswick)
Morris Museum (Morristown)
Newark Museum (Newark)
New Jersey State Museum (Trenton)

NEW MEXICO
New Mexico Museum of Natural History & Science (Albuquerque)
Meteorite Museum (University of New Mexico, Albuquerque)
Las Cruces Museum of Nature & Science (Las Cruces)
Miles Mineral Museum (Portales)
New Mexico Bureau of Geology Museum (Socorro)

NEW YORK
New York State Museum (Albany)
Buffalo Museum of Science (Buffalo)
Museum of the Earth (Ithaca)
American Museum of Natural History (New York City)

NORTH CAROLINA
North Carolina Museum of Natural Sciences (Raleigh)

NORTH DAKOTA
North Dakota Heritage Center & State Museum (Bismarck)

OHIO
Cincinnati Museum of Natural History & Science (Cincinnati)
Cleveland Museum of Natural History (Cleveland)
Limper Geology Museum (Oxford)

OKLAHOMA
Sam Noble Museum of Natural History (Norman)

OREGON
Rice Northwest Museum of Rocks and Minerals (Hillsboro)

PENNSYLVANIA
State Museum of Pennsylvania (Harrisburg)
The Academy of Natural Sciences of Drexel University (Philadelphia)
Carnegie Museum of Natural History (Pittsburgh)
Everhart Museum (Scranton)

RHODE ISLAND
Roger Williams Park Museum of Natural History (Providence)

SOUTH CAROLINA
The Charleston Museum (Charleston)
Mace Brown Museum of Natural History (College of Charleston, Charleston)
The Bob Campbell Geology Museum (Clemson)
McKissick Museum (Columbia)
South Carolina State Museum (Columbia)

SOUTH DAKOTA
South Dakota School of Mines & Technology Geology Museum (Rapid City)

TENNESSEE
McClung Museum of Natural History & Culture (Knoxville)

TEXAS
Texas Memorial Museum (Austin)
Perot Museum of Nature and Science (Dallas)
Fort Worth Museum of Science and History (Fort Worth)
Houston Museum of Natural Science (Houston)
Heard Natural Science Museum & Wildlife Sanctuary (McKinney)
Mayborn Museum (Waco)

UTAH
USU Geology Museum (Logan)
Clark Planetarium (Salt Lake City)
Natural History Museum of Utah (Salt Lake City)

VERMONT
The Perkins Geology Museum at the University of Vermont (Burlington)
Vermont Museum of Mining and Minerals (Grafton)

VIRGINIA
Virginia Tech Museum of Geosciences (Blacksburg)
Virginia Museum of Natural History (Martinsville)

WASHINGTON
Burke Museum of Natural History and Culture (Seattle)

WEST VIRGINIA
West Virginia Geological & Economic Survey Museum (Morgantown)

WISCONSIN
Earthaven Museum (Gillette)
University of Wisconsin Geology Museum (Madison)

WYOMING
Tate Geological Museum (Casper)
University of Wyoming Geological Museum (Laramie)

FURTHER READING

These books and websites have been useful in the creation of this book. To learn more about meteorites in general, please check them out.

BOOKS

Cressy, Frank. *From Weston to Creston: A Compendium of Witnessed US Meteorite Falls, 1807–2016*. Bakersfield, CA: Frank Cressy, 2016. This book highlights every meteorite fall in the United States up to 2016 and provides detailed insights and backstory on each one.

Norton, O. Richard. *Rocks from Space: Meteorites and Meteorite Hunters*. Missoula, MT: Mountain, 1998. This is a classic that covers all things related to meteorites.

Norton, O. Richard, and Lawrence Chitwood. *Field Guide to Meteors and Meteorites*. London: Springer, 2008. An excellent guide to the science of meteorites.

Notkin, Geoffrey. *Meteorite Hunting: How to Find Treasure from Space*. Tucson, AZ: Stanegate, 2011. A great book on meteorite hunting.

WEBSITES

AMERICAN METEOR SOCIETY: amsmeteors.org

This official site has information about various meteors and fireballs. It's also a good place to report your own sightings.

BUSECK CENTER FOR METEORITE STUDIES: meteorites.asu.edu

This website has a lot of useful information about meteorites, including short stories about specific meteorites.

COSMIC CONNECTION METEORITES: cosmicconnectionmeteorites.com

The website of Larry Atkins that features his adventures in meteorite hunting.

FALLING ROCKS: fallingrocks.com

The website of meteorite collector Dave Gheesling. Contains many insightful pictures and stories about meteorites, especially ones from Georgia.

KD METEORITES: kdmeteorites.com

This website run by Keith and Dana Jenkerson features their meteorite-hunting adventures and offers meteorites for sale.

METEORITE TIMES MAGAZINE: meteorite-times.com

Contains interesting articles about a variety of meteorites from around the world.

THE METEORITICAL BULLETIN DATABASE BY THE METEORITICAL SOCIETY: lpi.usra.edu/meteor

This searchable database has scientific information on every official meteorite. You can search by state, type, name, etc.

MILE HIGH METEORITES: mhmeteorites.com

This site of meteorite collector and dealer Matt Morgan has a lot of useful information about meteorites and great photos too.

PHOTO CREDITS

Unlisted photos are courtesy of the author.

Base maps by Jane Levy

Map symbols by Ethan Kocak

INTRODUCTORY PAGES

Goose Lake: Smithsonian Institution CC0: https://www.si.edu/object/geology-exhibits-natural-history-building-goose-lake-meteorite:siris_arc_402184

4 Vesta: NASA/JPL-Caltech/UCLA/MPS/DLR/IDA

Comet: Courtesy of Justin Starr Photography

Meteorite on Mars: NASA/JPL-Caltech/MSSS

Meteor: Courtesy of Mark Miller

Fusion Crust: Courtesy of Aaron Miller

Regmaglypts: Smithsonian Institution CC0: https://www.si.edu/object/eet-920290:nmnhmineralsciences_1025444

Oriented: Smithsonian Institution CC0: https://www.si.edu/object/gro-852010:nmnhmineralsciences_1023599

Density: Smithsonian Insitution CC0: https://www.si.edu/object/holbrook:nmnhmineralsciences_1014882

Fall: Courtesy of Aaron Miller

Find: Courtesy of Larry Atkins

Science: Smithsonian Institution CC0: https://www.si.edu/object/allende:nmnhmineralsciences_1017504

Crater: USGS

Strewn field: American Museum of Natural History Guide Leaflet – 1901: https://www.flickr.com/photos/internetarchivebookimages/14765713354/

Thin section: Smithsonian Institution CC0: https://www.si.edu/object/allende:nmnhmineralsciences_1041034

STATE PAGES

Alabama meteorite Sylacauga: Courtesy of the Alabama Museum of Natural History

Alabama meteorite Leighton: Photo by D. L. Schrader/ASU. Courtesy of the ASU Buseck Center for Meteorite Studies

Alaska meteorite Aggie Creek: Courtesy of Dustin Garth Stewart

Alaska meteorite Chilkoot: Photo by D. L. Schrader/ASU. Courtesy of the ASU Buseck Center for Meteorite Studies

Arizona Meteor Crater Picture: USGS

Arizona meteorite Canyon Diablo: Photo by author of NMNH specimen

Arizona meteorite Tucson Ring: Harris & Ewing. Library of Congress. 1938 or 1939. Call number: LC-H22-D- 7656 [P&P]. https://www.loc.gov/resource/hec.27531/

Arkansas meteorite Paragould: Courtesy of the University of Arkansas Museum

Arkansas meteorite Success: Smithsonian Institution CC0: https://www.si.edu/object/success:nmnhmineralsciences_1020562

Arkansas Success thin section: Smithsonian Institution CC0 - https://www.si.edu/object/success:nmnhmineralsciences_1041409

California meteorite Old Woman: Smithsonian Institution CC0: https://www.si.edu/object/old-woman:nmnhmineralsciences_1034844

California meteorite Creston: Courtesy of Aaron Miller

Colorado meteorite Johnstown: Courtesy of Matt Morgan, Mile High Meteorites

Colorado meteorite Elbert: Courtesy of Matt Morgan, Mile High Meteorites

Connecticut meteorite Weston: Courtesy of the Division of Mineralogy and Meteoritics; YPM MIN.100375, Peabody Museum of Natural History, Yale University, New Haven, Connecticut, USA; peabody.yale.edu. Photography by Lorenz, R. A., 2015.

Connecticut meteorite Wethersfield: Courtesy of the Division of Mineralogy and Meteoritics; YPM MIN. 101126, Peabody Museum of Natural History, Yale University, New Haven, Connecticut, USA; peabody.yale.edu. Photography by Sacco, W. K., 2005

Delaware landscape: Courtesy of Ashley Kennedy

Delaware page ventifact: Courtesy of Dr. Fred J. Calef III

Florida meteorite Osceola 1 & 2: Courtesy of Larry Atkins

Florida meteorite Grayton: Courtesy of anonymous

Georgia mailbox and meteorite Claxton: Courtesy of Dave Gheesling. The Falling Rocks Collection

Georgia meteorite Losttown: Photo by L. Garvie/ASU. Courtesy of the ASU Buseck Center for Meteorite Studies

Hawaii meteorite Honolulu: Courtesy of the Joachim Karl Meteorite Collection

Hawaii meteorite Honolulu thin section: Smithsonian Institution CC0 - https://www.si.edu/object/honolulu:nmnhmineralsciences_1040813

Hawaii meteorite Palolo Valley thin section: Smithsonian Institution CC0 - https://www.si.edu/object/palolo-valley:nmnhmineralsciences_1041506

Idaho meteorite Jerome: Courtesy of Martin Horejsi

Idaho meteorite Wilder: Courtesy of Martin Horejsi

Idaho meteorite Oakley: Photo by author of NMNH specimen

Illinois meteorite Park Forest: Courtesy of Matt Morgan, Mile High Meteorites

Illinois meteorite Park Forest thin section: Smithsonian Institution CCO- https://www.si.edu/object/park-forest:nmnhmineralsciences_1354835

Illinois meteorite Benld: Courtesy of the ASU Buseck Center for Meteorite Studies

Indiana meteorite Lafayette 1 & 2: Smithsonian Institution CC0: https://www.si.edu/object/lafayette-stone:nmnhmineralsciences_1370424

Indiana meteorite Hamlet: Courtesy of Matt Morgan, Mile High Meteorites

Iowa meteorite Homestead: Smithsonian Institution CC0: https://www.si.edu/object/homestead:nmnhmineralsciences_1013503

Iowa meteorite Estherville: Smithsonian Institution CC0: https://www.si.edu/object/estherville:nmnhmineralsciences_1033220

Kansas meteorite Brenham: Courtesy of KD Meteorites, Keith + Dana Jenkerson

Kansas meteorite Brenham 2: Smithsonian Institution CCO - https://www.si.edu/object/brenham:nmnhmineralsciences_1033427

Kansas meteorite Norton County: Courtesy of Matt Morgan, Mile High Meteorites

Kentucky meteorite Murray: Photo by D. L. Schrader/ASU. Courtesy of the ASU Buseck Center for Meteorite Studies

Kentucky meteorite Cumberland Falls: Smithsonian Institution CC0: https://www.si.edu/object/cumberland-falls:nmnhmineralsciences_1020994

Louisiana meteorite New Orleans: Photo by D. L. Schrader/ASU. Courtesy of the ASU Buseck Center for Meteorite Studies

Louisiana meteorite New Orleans other view: Courtesy of Martin Horejsi

Louisiana meteorite Greenwell Springs: Courtesy of Martin Horejsi

Maine meteorite Nobleborough: Photo by D. L. Schrader/ASU. Courtesy of the ASU Buseck Center for Meteorite Studies

Maine meteorite Andover: Courtesy of Matt Morgan, Mile High Meteorites

Maryland meteorite Nanjemoy: Photo by D. L. Schrader/ASU. Courtesy of the ASU Buseck Center for Meteorite Studies

Maryland meteorite St Mary's County: Smithsonian Institution CC0: https://www.si.edu/object/st-marys-county:nmnhmineralsciences_1041255

Massachusetts meteorite Barnstable: Courtesy of Steven J Amara Jr – Space Matter

Massachusetts meteorite Northampton: Courtesy of the Institute of Meteoritics at The University of New Mexico

Michigan meteorite Worden and car: Courtesy of Matt Morgan, Mile High Meteorites

Michigan meteorite Rose City: Smithsonian Institution CC0: https://www.si.edu/object/rose-city:nmnhmineralsciences_1014211

Minnesota meteorite Fisher: Courtesy of Matt Morgan, Mile High Meteorites

Minnesota meteorite Fisher thin section: Smithsonian Institution CC0: https://www.si.edu/object/fisher:nmnhmineralsciences_1040807

Minnesota meteorite Arlington: Courtesy of KD Meteorites, Keith + Dana Jenkerson

Mississippi meteorite Baldwyn complete: from G.P. Merrill's "A new meteoric stone from Baldwin, Mississippi." Proceedings of the US National Museum, no. 2578, vol 67. 1925.

Mississippi meteorite Palahatchie: from Frank Montgomery's "The Pelahatchie meteor, which passed over central Mississippi in the forenoon of October 17th, 1910." Monthly Weather Review, January, 1911, page 16.

Mississippi meteorite Baldwyn samples: Photo by D. L. Schrader/ASU. Courtesy of the ASU Bueseck Center for Meteorite Studies

Missouri meteorite Conception Junction and close-up: Courtesy of KD Meteorites, Keith + Dana Jenkerson

Montana meteorite Twodot: Courtesy of Martin Horejsi

Montana meteorite Choteau and close-up: Courtesy of KD Meteorites, Keith + Dana Jenkerson

Nebraska meteorite Sioux County: Courtesy of the ASU Bueseck Center for Meteorite Studies

Nevada meteorite Battle Mountain: Courtesy of the ASU Bueseck Center for Meteorite Studies

Nevada meteorite Battle Mountain field pic: Courtesy of Larry Atkins

Nevada meteorite Quinn Canyon: Smithsonian Institution CC0: https: www.si.edu/object/quinn-canyon:nmnhmineralsciences_1022223

New Hampshire landscapes: Courtesy of Jeanne Timmons

New Hampshire meteor-wrong: Courtesy of Zoltán Sylvester

New Jersey meteorite Deal: Courtesy of the Joachim Karl Meteorite Collection

New Jersey meteor-wrong: Courtesy of Scott Mermelstein

New Mexico meteorite Glorieta Mountain backlit: Courtesy of KD Meteorites, Keith + Dana Jenkerson

New York meteorite Peekskill and car: Courtesy of Professor Williman Menke and Professor Mark Anders, Columbia University

New York meteorite Schenectady: Courtesy of miSci, Museum of Innovation and Science

North Carolina meteorite Farmville: Smithsonian Institution CC0: https://www.si.edu/object/farmville:nmnhmineralsciences_1033650

North Carolina meteorite Moore County: Photo by D. L. Schrader/ASU. Courtesy of the ASU Bueseck Center for Meteorite Studies

North Dakota meteorite Richardton: Courtesy of Matt Morgan, Mile High Meteorites

North Dakota meteorite Richardton thin section: Smithsonian Institution CC0: https://www.si.edu/object/richardton:nmnhmineralsciences_1041572

North Dakota meteorite Bowesmont thin section: Smithsonian Institution CC0: https://www.si.edu/object/bowesmont:nmnhmineralsciences_1040748

Ohio meteorite New Concord: Courtesy of the ASU Bueseck Center for Meteorite Studies

Oklahoma meteorite Lake Murray: Courtesy of KD Meteorites, Keith + Dana Jenkerson

Oklahoma meteorite Crescent: Courtesy of the ASU Bueseck Center for Meteorite Studies

Oklahoma meteorite Beaver thin section: Smithsonian Institution CC0: https://www.si.edu/object/beaver:nmnhmineralsciences_1370307

Oregon meteorite Willamette 1: CC0: 1906 postcard from Brück & Son https://commons.wikimedia.org/wiki/File:08115-Oregon_City-1906-Meteorite_discovered_in_Oregon_City-Br%C3%BCck_%26_Sohn_Kunstverlag.jpg

Oregon meteorite Willamette 2: page 9 of "General Guide to the exhibition halls of the American Museum of Natural History" 1911. American Museum of Natural History. New York. From https://flickr.com/photos/126377022@N07/14764258155

Oregon meteorite Salem: Courtesy of the Cascadia Meteorite Laboratory at Portland State University

Pennsylvania meteorite Black Moshannan Park: Courtesy of the Joachim Karl Meteorite Collection

Pennsylvania meteorite Mount Joy fragment: Courtesy of Martin Horejsi

Pennsylvania meteorite Mount Joy cross section: Courtesy of the Adams County Historical Society / Gettysburg Beyond the Battle Museum

Rhode Island beach: Juliancolton – public domain https://commons.wikimedia.org/wiki/File:Beach_house_at_Misquamicut_Beach,_Rhode_Island.JPG

South Carolina meteorite Bishopville: Photo by L. Garvie/ASU. Courtesy of the ASU Bueseck Center for Meteorite Studies

South Dakota meteorite Bath: Courtesy of Matt Morgan, Mile High Meteorites

South Dakota meteorite Centerville thin section: Smithsonian Institution CC0: https://www.si.edu/object/centerville:nmnhmineralsciences_1041601

Tennessee meteorite Petersburg: Photo by L. Garvie/ASU. Courtesy of the ASU Bueseck Center for Meteorite Studies

Tennessee meteorite Charlotte: Photo by D. L. Schrader/ASU. Courtesy of the
ASU Buseck Center for Meteorite Studies

Tennessee meteorite Maryville thin section: Smithsonian Institution CC0:
https://www.si.edu/object/maryville:nmnhmineralsciences_1041773

Texas meteorite Odessa: Courtesy of Matt Morgan, Mile High Meteorites

Texas meteorite Ash Creek: Courtesy of the ASU Buseck Center for Meteorite Studies

Texas meteorite Pena Blanca Spring: Courtesy of Matt Morgan, Mile High
Meteorites

Utah meteorite Drum Mountain: Photo by author of NMNH specimen

Utah meteorite Ioka: Smithsonian Institution CC0: https://www.si.edu/object/
ioka:nmnhmineralsciences_1021393

Vermont landscape: Courtesy of Alana Quinn

Virginia meteorite Richmond: Photo by D. L. Schrader/ASU. Courtesy of the
ASU Buseck Center for Meteorite Studies

Virginia meteorite 2: Photo by author of NMNH specimen

Virginia meteorite Sharps: Smithsonian Institution CC0: https://www.si.edu/
object/sharps:nmnhmineralsciences_1041859

Washington meteorite Waterville: Courtesy of the Douglas County Historical
Society Museum

Washington meteorite Withrow: Courtesy of the Douglas County Historical
Society Museum

West Virginia meteorite Landes: Photo by D. L. Schrader/ASU. Courtesy of the
ASU Buseck Center for Meteorite Studies

West Virginia meteorite Jenny's Creek: Photo by D. L. Schrader/ASU. Courtesy
of the ASU Buseck Center for Meteorite Studies

Wisconsin meteorite Mifflin: Courtesy of Larry Atkins

Wyoming meteorite Albin: Courtesy of KD Meteorites, Keith + Dana Jenkerson

Wyoming meteorite Torrington: Photo by D. L. Schrader/ASU. Courtesy of the
ASU Buseck Center for Meteorite Studies

ACKNOWLEDGMENTS

This book would not have been possible without the
recommendations, contacts, information, editing, and goodwill of
the following people:

Dr. Carl Agee	James Holstein	Aaron Miller
Steven J. Amara Jr.	Dr. Martin Horejsi	Mark Miller
Mark Anders	Chris Hunter	Matt Morgan
Larry Atkins	Melinda Hutson	Sean T. Murray
Dr. Fred J. Calef III	Dana Jenkerson	Dr. Stefan Nicolescu
Ann Charles	Keith Jenkerson	Alana Quinn
Frank Cressy	Joachim Karl	Alex Ruzicka
Danielle D. Farmer	Moritz Karl	Devin Schrader
Alison Fong	Ashley Kennedy	Heather Spence
John Friel	Ethan Kocak	Justin Starr
Erin Gredell	Celeste Labedz	Dustin Stewart
Tracee Groff	Jane Levy	Mary Suter
Beth Ha	William Menke	Zoltán Sylvester
Jenifer Holcomb	Scott Mermelstein	Jeanne Timmons

INDEX